An Accidental Canadian

Margaret Wente

An Accidental Canadian

Reflections on My Home and (Not) Native Land

HarperCollins*PublishersLtd*

HarperCollins Publishers Ltd
2 Bloor Street East, 20th Floor
Toronto, Ontario, Canada
M4W 1A8

www.harpercollins.ca

Library and Archives Canada Cataloguing in Publication

Wente, Margaret, 1950–
An accidental Canadian : reflections on my home and (not) native land / Margaret Wente. – 1st ed.

ISBN 0-00-200798-3

I. Title.

FC97.W45 2004   081   C2004-904576-8

HC 9 8 7 6 5 4 3 2 1

Printed and bound in the United States
Set in Minion

FOR IAN

Contents

Acknowledgments

This book was conceived by my friend and editor, Hugh Brewster. He talked me into it one winter day as he stood in my country kitchen in his long underwear. Under the circumstances, I could hardly refuse. His good judgment and good humour made this project a pleasure.

I want to express my thanks and gratitude to my employer, *The Globe and Mail,* and to my editors at the paper, for giving me the best platform in the country. I'm very lucky to work with such talented and dedicated people.

Thanks also to Beverley Slopen for her advice, counsel and friendship, to Andy Barrie for the video, to Phillip Andres for taking care of certain pressing details, to the jacket designer, Sharon Kish, and to photographer Ian Brewster. At HarperCollins, thanks to Iris Tupholme, Kevin Hanson and freelance editor Stephanie Fysh.

An Accidental Canadian

Confessions of an Accidental Canadian

I grew up in a Wonder Bread suburb of Chicago in the 1950s. Every kid I knew was pale pink, and all the families were nuclear. My world looked like the illustrations in the Dick and Jane books. Everyone was middle class and voted Republican, except my dad, who was regarded as a colourful radical. The only dark-skinned person I ever saw up close was my grandma's cleaning lady, who didn't live in our town. I never met a single foreigner. (The U.S. government called them "aliens.") In our town, diversity was supplied by a few Jewish families, a lady who played a harp and some unfortunate people who lived in apartments.

When I was a kid, we would celebrate the fourth of July (or, as Americans spell it, the Fourth) with a trip to Soldier Field, where we sang "The Star-Spangled Banner" at the top of our lungs with thousands of other Americans, hands planted across our hearts. There were magnificent fireworks, which always ended with a dazzling American flag depicted in red, white and blue sparklers. I wore my favourite dress, which was white with red and blue trim. My little sister Sally wore a matching dress.

Americans wear their patriotism with pride, for all to see. "Live free or die," is the state motto of New Hampshire. This display of national confidence makes Canadians cringe. If we had to come up with a new motto, it would probably be "Canada. Not bad! / Le Canada. Pas mal!"

In the United States, no one ponders what it is to be an American. They never go in search of the elusive American identity. The question simply never occurs. When you are a member of the world's dominant culture, your identity is secure.

Like most Americans in Canada, I got here accidentally. This lack of intent makes us unique among all immigrant groups. We didn't come here to escape repression, intolerance or poverty, or to make a better life for our children. We were not chasing an ideal of freedom. We came because we got a job here or fell in love with someone or wanted to escape the draft, and Canada was a reasonably pleasant place to live. If you're from Chicago, Toronto looks more culturally familiar than Dallas.

Unlike other immigrants, we didn't have to make a big commitment either. We never had to struggle with the language, take ESL, adapt ourselves to foreign ways or leave our families far behind across an ocean. We didn't have to work at menial jobs because our credentials were no good, or adjust to life as a visible minority. As immigrants, we are totally assimilated from the moment we arrive, and totally invisible.

Most of us never dreamed we'd stay for life. Canada was just another stop, like Atlanta or Seattle. Then one day you realize you've been here fifteen years and have put down roots, and you're tired of paying taxes without voting, so you decide to swear allegiance to the Queen. And the day the citizenship judge pronounces you Canadian, along with a hundred other people from all corners of the earth, you're caught unawares by how emotional and proud you feel. She tells you to shake hands with the people next to you, your fellow citizens, and you're overwhelmed with love for all these strangers. You also feel like a little bit of a fraud, because you know all of them had a far longer, harder journey here than you did.

Americans who've chosen Canada tend to be tremendously self-congratulatory. Some of us are even more smug and condescending toward the United States than native-born Canadians are. The crime! The guns! The arrogance! The racism! The death penalty! The quagmire in Iraq! The forty-five million people who don't have health insurance! The moron in the White House! The fat people you see at Disney World! The Christian Right! The banality of popular culture! These sins are proof of our wisdom in converting, as well as automatic proof of Canada's superior virtue.

I used to bad-mouth the U.S. too. But now that bad-mouthing the U.S. is Canada's second most popular national sport, I am puzzled. Why are we so sensitive about bashing other cultures but so quick to bash America's? Why do we teach our kids that stereotyping people is dreadfully wrong, then gleefully stereotype Americans? Why do we condemn intolerance except when it's directed against the most tolerant and democratic country in the world?

I can hear the Canadian chorus now. Because they're arrogant. Because they're bullies. Because they're warmongering crusaders. Because the morons in charge of the country are either immoral or foolhardy, and probably both. Because they don't give a damn what the rest of the world thinks. Because individual Americans are fine—it's their government and policies we can't stand, even though individual Americans more or less support them. Because they're entirely too powerful for everybody's good.

So here's a question. If we had to choose another country to be entirely too powerful, which one would we prefer? And would we rather live next to them instead?

One of America's best traits is its own habit of self-criticism and debate. Nothing Canadians say about it is worse than what many Americans say about themselves. And one of Canada's worst traits is its smugness. It's easy to snipe from the sidelines when you've got nothing on the line yourself. Sniping contributes to our national self-esteem. It helps us forget that we don't, after all, count for very much in the world, and that we need them far more than they need us.

We think that America's sense of national pride is built on a web of self-delusions. But so is our own. We have the finest health care system in the world, except that we have no idea how we're going to pay for it two years from now. We have a vibrant parliamentary democracy, where the same party has been in power forever. We have wonderful, liveable cities, if you don't mind the gridlock in Toronto, the shooting galleries in Vancouver, the general shabbiness and neglect and . . . oh, never mind. I love this country, I really do. It has beauty that makes you feel as if you're standing next to God. It gave me opportunities I never dreamed I'd have, and for those I shall be forever thankful.

In 1964, my mother, now divorced, married a Canadian, and we all moved from Dick-and-Jane-land to Toronto. We landed in Don Mills, on the edge of a city that was just about to utterly transform itself. In honour of my new life, I dyed my mouse-brown hair platinum blond and started spelling my first name Peggi, with a big round circle above the *i*.

In those days Toronto was a straitlaced Protestant provincial town where every place closed tight on Sunday and the movie theatres played "God Save the Queen" after the last screening. But deference was definitely on the wane and most people would sneak out during the closing credits so that they wouldn't have to stand at attention.

Even so, Toronto was by far the most exotic place I'd ever been. It even had a café where you could buy espresso, a drink I'd never heard of. In Yorkville, Gordon Lightfoot and Joni Mitchell were playing in the coffee houses. The city was full of allure for a girl from the suburbs of America. It was a good place to reinvent yourself.

The world was about to reinvent Toronto, too. The immigrants came flooding in, and by the end of the decade the city was on a roll. My future husband moved here, part of the wave of Anglo refugees from Montreal. Toronto was the place to be if you wanted to work in music, entertainment, TV or publishing. It was Canada's New York—a magnet for the best and brightest.

After I finished university in the States (where they'd let you in after Grade 12), I had to make the biggest decision of my life: Canada or the United States? The U.S. was in a dark phase, torn apart by the awful politics of Vietnam. Canada was in a good phase, newly vibrant, cosmopolitan, open to the world. It was a no-brainer. I chose Canada.

Crossing the border these days, former Americans with Canadian passports are sometimes greeted with suspicion by U.S. immigration officers. Why don't we have an American passport? they ask. Have we actually renounced our citizenship and, if so, why? Their voices are always full of reproach. We know what they're thinking. How could we, born and bred in the greatest nation on earth, deny our heritage? Either we must have something to hide or else we are disloyal. Or maybe both.

"Do you ever think of going home?" people here sometimes ask me. I think they mean, You've got a choice, so why don't you live where taxes are lower, salaries are higher and winters are shorter? Or maybe they mean that since I stick up for the U.S. so much, it's odd that I don't live there. My answer is the one all immigrants give. For better and for worse, I am home.

Home is a neighbourhood in Toronto that is pleasantly diverse. Up the street is a brand-new, million-dollar faux French chateau. Across the street is a city-owned apartment building. For thirty years we boasted perhaps the only restaurant in the world that served both haggis and Wiener schnitzel (the ecumenical result, I believe, of a cross-cultural marriage).

For more than a century, the boardwalk at the bottom of my street has been a summer playground for the sweltering citizens of the city. Now it's the crossroads of the world. On Canada Day, it looks like a poster for UN Day. Along the boardwalk, the teenage boys and girls hold hands and kiss, defying all the lines of culture and colour. Do their parents know? Probably not. Under the trees, three-generation families from Pakistan and Bangladesh come to picnic, nap and spend the day. At night we watch the fireworks, which never include a display of the flag.

Not too long from now, I hope, most people in this city will not be black or white, Asian or Caucasian, but a cappuccino-coloured blend of the entire human race. I'm eager for the day when the census people will have to throw out their questions about ethnic origins because they will be meaningless. Perhaps our children's children will be amazed that such things once mattered.

Reflecting on the state of our nation usually makes me cranky, but two things always cheer me up. One is walking on the boardwalk on a summer weekend. The other is talking to cab drivers. They are the most patriotic people you will ever meet and, unlike native-born Canadians, are not shy about saying so. Most come from countries where there is no ice and snow, but they're all serious Leafs fans. They all think Canada is the greatest nation in the world, even if it lets them down sometimes.

"I was a journalist in Bangladesh," one cab driver told me. His name was Muhammad Ali. He had applied to every newspaper in Toronto, but no one would hire him. And so he writes for little papers that will take his work for free. He also was the proud father of a week-old firstborn son. What did they name him? I asked. "Michael," he beamed.

Near the subway stop where I drop my husband off, the Muslim women in their head coverings and ankle-length skirts walk their thoroughly Canadian children to school. Sometimes you see women shrouded in burkas, walking three steps behind their husbands. A few years from now some of their kids will be sneaking down to the boardwalk on a summer weekend to show off their navel rings and illicitly hold hands with other people's children—maybe yours. Thankfully, official multiculturalism will never survive the assault of unofficial love.

Canada is still a raw, new country, and that's its greatest strength. Newcomers to Britain can never really be British, and newcomers to France can never really be French. But in Canada we're almost all newcomers. Our national identity isn't in our national roots, which are very shallow, or in our national health care system, which is disintegrating, or in our national quarrel with the Americans. It is in our miraculous ability to make room for newcomers like me, and to let us build a home.

I have only one wish for us, one modest little wish. Can't we be a little bit more patriotic?

Although Canadians find this trait alarming, I've come to admire our neighbours for their unapologetic love of country. They plant their hands over their hearts and say the Pledge of Allegiance as if they really mean it. We can barely mumble a few bars of "O Canada," and whenever we are called upon to do so we sound half-hearted and embarrassed, like sullen adolescents who've been made to go to church and pray out loud or to recite a really corny poem.

My one wish for my home and not-native land is for us to get over that. I admit our national anthem is not the best. But we should grow up and belt it out with pride, as a way of giving thanks that, by some stupendous happy accident, we have the good luck to belong to the most fortunate nation on earth.

Chapter One

Our Icons

What sets Canada apart from all other nations? I would start with our spectacular geography, our vast and empty spaces, our two founding nations, our tolerance for everyone from everywhere, our remarkably bloodless national history. In my more surly moods I might mention our extraordinary fondness for government, which has given us perhaps the highest ratio of politicians and civil servants to citizens than just about any place on earth.

Then there are the people and institutions that hold a special place in our national consciousness. They have helped to shape our sense of ourselves. They exemplify our greatest political and cultural achievements (or so we believe), and they make us proud. That's what Pierre Trudeau, hockey and Margaret Atwood have in common. All are national icons.

Pierre Trudeau's death in 2000 plunged the country into mourning. For a politician who had long been in retirement and who had been reviled and loathed during his last years in office, it was an extraordinary outpouring of emotion. This outpouring did not extend to most of the West, where Trudeau remains the greatest villain of a rapacious, eastern-dominated central government. But for lots of people of my generation, Trudeau was our JFK—a leader with charisma, a gorgeous wife, handsome kids and a matchless sense of style. He was our leader when we came of age, began taking pride in our new flag and grew more self-confident than we've been before or since. He brought us the idea of the Just Society and bequeathed us the Charter of Rights and Freedoms. Whenever people are asked to vote for the greatest Canadian of all time, Trudeau comes at or near the top.

You need only one guess to name Canada's greatest national institution. Hint: it's not Parliament. Immigrants like me know that you're safer spitting on the flag than questioning the glory that is our game. Fortunately for nationalists, hockey assimilates us all. In a brand-new Punjabi subdivision of Toronto, brown-skinned boys from broiling lands play pickup with balls and sticks on summer nights. This is one tradition that multiculturalism will never erode.

Around the time that Trudeau became PM, CanLit came into flower. We may have flopped at TV and movies, but we sure could write. Perhaps that's because novelists and poets don't need to go to Hollywood to make a living. The undisputed queen of CanLit is Margaret Atwood, author of countless novels—most with bitter women and unhappy endings—and winner of countless international literary prizes. Maybe she's the greatest writer in the history of Canada, or maybe not (personally, my money's on Alice Munro). No matter. She's fierce. You don't cross her.

Here's my own quite personal take on these three national icons. Please don't stone me if you disagree. What do I know? I'm just an immigrant.

Our Most Seductive Leader

It was a dinner like a hundred others, in support of I don't remember what. What I do remember is the arrival of Pierre Elliott Trudeau, a small, sparely built man with a very large aura. All heads in the roomful of notables and dignitaries turned toward him. He must have been seventy-seven then. Someone introduced us. "Ah, Margaret," he murmured, pressing his lips to the back of my hand. "I do so enjoy your columns."

My knees turned to goo.

For all his time in public life Pierre Trudeau was a master of seduction, of both men and women alike, on both large and small scales. He made a nation fall slavishly in love with him for a while, and even in old age his charm endured. "He was an attractive, interesting and possibly dangerous man," said Iona Campagnolo, a long-time Liberal colleague. "Most women like men like that."

Trudeau was the first (and perhaps the last) Canadian politician to have groupies. In 1967, girls like me turned out in hordes to scream and beg for autographs. Politicians are supposed to be professionally seductive, but most are as seductive as sawdust. Most are either backslapping Rotarians, greasy car salesmen or earnest nerds. The only other Canadian politician with a Trudeau-sized magnetic force field was Peter Lougheed. And the only other great Canadian ladies' man is Leonard Cohen. Like Trudeau, he's the thinking woman's heartthrob, a sensual intellectual with a strong ascetic streak. (Never underestimate the sex appeal of a Jesuit or a Buddhist.) Both achieved spectacular success snubbing convention and bourgeois values. Both could ravish a woman with words, and both had emotionally elusive personalities. They are men of masks and performance, who promise intimacy but never, finally, deliver; private men who will not, hard as you knock, ever really let you in. They cannot be domesticated. Women are suckers for men like these, and men like these always break lots of women's hearts.

"He was a very distant man," says Trudeau's son Sacha. Sacha and Justin, the two surviving sons, are among the few people who ever saw the man without his masks. To hear them speak so fondly yet so truthfully of him feels shockingly intimate.

Yet intimacy was the one great gift that eluded their surpassingly gifted father. It was too dangerous, perhaps. Intimacy makes you weak. Trudeau learned from an early age to overcome whatever was weak, to temper his body and his mind so that they would become hard and invulnerable.

He learned these lessons from his mother, and from the Jesuits.

"The Jesuits have this, you know," said Sacha. "You take what you have and you thrust it out as hard as you can and what's left is what's true."

Pierre was a frail and scrawny child who did sports to build himself up. His parents' union was contradictory and conflicted and emblematically Canadian. His mother, Grace, was a disciplined Anglo. His father, Charlie, was a flamboyant self-made man who made a fortune from gas stations. Charlie was a ladies' man, a loud and sociable guy who spent most nights with his cronies, drinking and smoking and playing cards.

When Pierre was fifteen, his hard-living father dropped dead. Grace maintained it was Charlie's habits that killed him, and she made sure Pierre, the oldest son, did not miss the lesson of his father's dissolution. "You have to lead a more careful life. Disciplined. Healthy. Pure," recalled Justin.

Pierre was both a sensualist, like his father, and austere, like his mother. But it was his mother he revered. "He spoke of her with such respect and awe," said Sacha. "She was an exceedingly wise woman."

And so Pierre learned at an early age to keep the sensuality firmly in check, to never lose control, to always be the seducer, never the seduced. He became Canada's leading ladies' man, and courted many leading ladies. But the press, he warned, had no place in the bedroom of the prime minister, and his many affairs remained tantalizingly private. "If you're entitled to pry into my private affairs, I don't see why I couldn't be entitled to pry into yours," he told reporters, with that mix of playfulness and menace they came to know so well.

In all his life, he lost his heart to a woman only once. He lost it to a girl thirty years younger, and she broke it.

Margaret Trudeau was all emotion and no reason, all feeling

and no thinking, all exhibitionism and no reserve. She was as different from Pierre in her way as his father had been from his mother. It was a supreme romantic folly. In the one emotionally reckless moment of his life, he doomed them both to the exquisite private hell of a marriage that was cursed by temperamental incompatibility. They were not Venus and Mars—they belonged to different galaxies.

And when she ran away, after three babies and six years, the wreck of their marriage was public property. "He loved Margaret very deeply," said Trudeau's former press secretary Patrick Gossage. "It was obvious he suffered a lot. We kept up this fiction that he was fine, but he was hurting a lot. He really adored her and I think he felt very betrayed."

He suffered in silence. She told the world. "He couldn't give up his work for me, and therefore . . . we couldn't stay together," she confessed on national television. "I think I've decided that he's not the man for me."

In thirty-five years of life before the cameras, there are only a few glimpses of the man without the mask, and hardly any moments of self-revelation. One of those came during a fireside chat, late in his time in office, with a young female (no coincidence) TV interviewer. "When I was younger, I emphasized the importance of not taking myself too seriously, not taking other people too seriously," he reflected. "It might have been a bit of a pose or a defensive mechanism—a kind of hedging against possible failure. If I'd fail, it wasn't all that serious."

He made sure he would never fail at romance again. After Margaret left him, his broken heart hardened. He entertained spectacular beauties at Harrington Lake and read Teilhard de Chardin to Liona Boyd by moonlight. At seventy-two, he had a child with an accomplished single woman named Deborah Coyne. They named their daughter Sarah. No one howled in derision or disgust, or chewed over the morality of geriatric parenting. The *Globe*'s Brian Gable drew a cartoon showing a man at a restaurant pointing to Trudeau at the next table. "I'll have what he's having," he tells the waiter. And we all secretly envied Deborah Coyne, too.

But after Margaret, he kept his heart for the three boys he raised to men.

"Family and us were a way for him to know himself in a deep and not-so-rational way," said Sacha. "I think that was very important to him. That was one of the few things that was true to him and real to him. Us. His family."

"People perceived him as tough and arrogant," said Justin. "We would perceive him as strong and disciplined."

The mask of the warrior-philosopher was to drop in public only once again, at the funeral of his son Michel. And there he was for all the world to see. The strength all gone, and the heart, so guarded, broken forever.

At his own funeral, the world stopped for a while as Justin spoke, and then we all, like him, dissolved into tears. He melted the most hardened hearts. Who knew Pierre Trudeau had such a son?

Modern politics doesn't mix with the values that shaped Pierre Trudeau's nature. It's impossible to imagine him pandering to the flutters of the latest focus groups, submitting to the image-makers or shaping policy according to the popularity polls. His intellectual rigour, his disdain for commerce and the marketplace and his rejection of cheap political opportunism would automatically disqualify him from leading any major party today.

Nor is it possible to imagine any politician today so indifferent to the trappings of power, so supremely, serenely inner-directed.

In the days after Trudeau's death, he surprised us all over again with what we hadn't known about him. He surprised us with his bottomless tenderness toward his children, and with his religiosity. This most rational and analytical of men was devoted above all to Justin, Sacha, Michel and Sarah, and to God.

It's unnerving, that faith. It came from a tradition of high-church intellectualism that has almost died out and is almost incomprehensible to worldly children of a secular age like ours. He used to slip into the back pew of the church for Sunday mass, and read Bible verses to his children. His spirituality was nothing like the phony public piety we require of modern leaders to signify they are moral men. It was quite private. And it gave the ancient ritual of the mass and the incense, the Latin hymns and the priests' robes, an overwhelming power.

Pierre Trudeau's sense of morality was Gallic and aristocratic, not English and bourgeois. There was a whiff of François Mitterrand to his last rites, with the public appearance of his daughter, Sarah, and her mother, to say nothing of assorted former mistresses. The American public would never stand for such irregularities at the funeral of a national leader, and the American media would make a scandal of it. We just cried.

Some of Trudeau's private values made for ruinous public policies. His contempt for business and the marketplace (or was it indifference?) was a disaster for Canada. He was a great man with dreadful economic ideas—the mirror image, perhaps, of Brian Mulroney. But he also understood that capitalism is innately Darwinian, and needs to be kept in check by an ethic of social justice.

I settled here for good in the Trudeau years because I thought that Canada was, on the whole, a more civil and more tolerant place. And so it still is, and that is a large part of Pierre Trudeau's legacy.

Alas, Pierre never did ask me to slip up to his suite or offer to read me passages from Teilhard de Chardin. And so, unlike Liona Boyd, I have no tell-all revelations to offer up in my memoirs—just the memory of one seductive kiss, and a perfectly foolish romantic fantasy about what might have been.

Can a Canadian Hate Hockey?

I don't really hate hockey. It's just that I never got the hang of it. To me, it looks like a lot of goons bashing at each other. Half the time you can't even see the puck. Baseball is more my kind of game. You can watch little kids playing baseball in the park without freezing to death. Baseball is a game of endless summer. Hockey is a game of endless winter. Baseball players have more teeth, and they have uniforms that allow you to contemplate their manly physiques. The World Series sensibly ends before the snow flies. But the hockey season hangs on forever. In Toronto, it can be hot enough outside to fry an egg, and it's still the quarter-finals. What kind of game is that?

When Canada beat Russia back in 1972, the nation went nuts. As it happens, I remember exactly where I was when we scored the winning goal. I was watching the game at the office, just like everybody else. I'd been hired right out of university as a book publicist, and my very first assignment was a book about the Canada–Russia hockey series. The coach of the Canadian team had been signed up to write it (or at least to pretend he had). "Maybe this means we'll sell more books," I said when we won. Little did I know what I was in for.

When the famous coach came to Toronto a few weeks later to launch his book, he was mobbed. My job was to organize a press conference for him. I had never organized a press conference before. In fact, I'd never even been to one. It was a shambles. The room was way too small, and all the sports reporters shouted their questions all at once. They were furious because I had no idea about deadlines. Afterward, the famous coach took pity on me and took me to a bar, where he was welcomed the same way that the Americans had welcomed the first astronaut who returned from space. People begged for his autograph. I knew I should make small talk with him about hockey, but I couldn't think of a single thing to say.

The hockey book sold more than all the Canadian novels published that year put together.

My other brush with hockey fame came a few years later, when I fell into conversation with a man while I was waiting for my luggage at the airport. He too was a hockey coach. I had no idea he was the coach of the greatest hockey team in Canada, or that he coached Wayne Gretzky, the greatest player in the history of the game. He was friendly and asked me on a date, so a week later I went out with him. I can't say it was much fun. I had never heard of Bobby Orr, and he had never heard of Margaret Atwood. We parted in a state of mutual bafflement. I never bothered telling any of my girlfriends that I'd gone out with him, because they wouldn't be impressed. They had no idea who he was either. But the men—well, they looked at me with sudden new respect.

Of course I *do* know who Don Cherry is. He's the creepy loudmouth in the awful shirts. Whenever I stumble across him by mistake, I change the channel as fast as possible. But millions of Canadians do the opposite. They tune in during the breaks. Sometimes *Hockey Night in Canada* gets higher ratings during Coach's Corner than during the actual game. Don Cherry is our national id. He can get away with saying things nobody else is allowed to anymore. When a female spectator was hit by a puck, he said, "Whenever a fan gets hit by a puck, it's always the same. Some woman, sitting there yapping." (This comment, of course, did not cause a national outcry and the insertion of an eight-second delay in the broadcast. It took a comment about "Europeans and French guys" to do that.)

My husband and I are a mixed marriage. He grew up in the Eastern Townships. His hero was Rocket Richard. Like every other boy, he grew up playing hockey, which gave him a keen appreciation of sportsmanship and the class system. Instead of the Habs and the Leafs, there were the English Protestants, the French Protestants, the English Catholics, the French Catholics and the private-school kids, who came from Westmount and were referred to by the locals as the Pablum boys. Hockey's in his blood.

So he was less than thrilled when I leaped to the defence of a little old lady called Nadja Ciuriak.

Perhaps you don't remember Nadja. Back in the winter of '02 she was the most hated woman in Canada. Her problem was that she publicly attacked Canada's most sacred national institution—street hockey.

For years, a bunch of local kids had been playing road hockey right in front of Ms. Ciuriak's house in Hamilton. Stray balls would bounce onto her lawn and hit her sister's car. Large boys would run after them, and often came close to trampling her tulips. She asked the boys to move their game up the street, but their father told the boys to ignore her. She complained again. No luck. She summoned the police, but they came and went away. Finally, she took the dad to court for violating the bylaw against playing hockey on the street.

Ms. Ciuriak is an immigrant. She didn't understand the sacred place of hockey in Canadian mythology. And so, instead of attracting sympathy for trying to protect her tulips, she was vilified from coast to coast for being cruel to patriotic little boys. Why did she come here, people said angrily, if she didn't want to adopt the Canadian way of life?

The neighbours were bad enough. The media were worse.

Most news editors are red-blooded jocks, and they turned Ms. Ciuriak into Public Enemy Number One. In their view, boyhood itself was at risk. The news editors devoted more air time to Ms. Ciuriak's day in court than to the war on terror, and they cast her in the role of the terrorists. When she lost her case, they gleefully ran footage of the neighbourhood boys waving their hockey sticks in triumph.

"We just want to play without someone calling the cops," said the gloating dad, who claimed to be a one-man saviour of street sports.

On phone-in shows and letters pages, outraged Canadian males cross-checked the foreign lady against the boards. "You and your bigoted, mean, petty attitudes are the reason so many teens become problem adults," said one outraged citizen. Others accused her of fostering not only juvenile delinquency, but also obesity, by discouraging exercise. "Perhaps we should backtrack to Salem and resurrect the dunking chair," suggested an aroused hockey fan.

The story about street hockey wasn't really about little boys. It was about our national identity. "Hockey is Canada's national pastime," the patriots reminded us. One local politician, who said he wished more boys would grow up playing road hockey just as he had, said he hoped the case would "rekindle our recognition of the importance of Canadian traditions." The poor lady was lucky she wasn't burned at the stake. "People involved with hockey seem to be mental cases," observed Ms. Ciuriak.

As an immigrant and a woman myself, I think she's got a point. Personally, I think that instead of promoting manly citizenship, hockey really promotes goonery, loutishness and diminished mental capacity—especially among hockey dads. The hockey father who fought Ms. Ciuriak, for example, has taught his sons that being rude to your neighbour and ignoring the law can make you a big hero and get you on national TV.

What other lessons do kids learn? Hockey is a sport where they send their big star back out to play after he's had his seventh concussion. He says he's fine, but how would he know? His brain has turned to scrambled eggs.

If hockey players don't start out as toothless morons, they'll probably wind up that way. And we won't even mention the addle-headed fans, who'd rather sweat through endless play-offs every June in front of the TV than get a life. Hockey does not promote civic engagement. It destroys it.

But it's unwise to say these things out loud. Whenever I write something mean about our national sport there is an avalanche of letters to the editor, all demanding that I be fired. You'd be safer stomping on the flag.

"Hockey, per se, is obviously a big part of what makes us *us*," wrote the *Globe*'s star sportswriter, Stephen Brunt. Like my husband, all sportswriters played road hockey forty years ago with nothing but simple lumps of snow to mark the goalposts. Today, the kids on my street play road hockey with real nets and $200 pairs of in-line skates. But there's no point trying to argue with a myth. Whenever I ask my husband to please explain the charms of hockey to me, he gets a certain misty look in his eyes and launches into rhapsodies about playing shinny as a boy back in Lennoxville, Quebec. Those were the magical times, when all the different teams, the English and the French, the Catholics and the Protestants, would come together every winter on the ice in order to beat the crap out of each other. Those were the days when he learned the true meaning of what it was to be Canadian.

The Queen of CanLit

Watch what you say about Margaret Atwood. She has spies everywhere. It is practically illegal to write anything rude about her or to wonder if she really is the greatest writer of our time. But really. Did you try to get through *The Blind Assassin*? I tried. And so did countless others. It won the Booker Prize. I didn't get it. It turned out that I was not alone.

One day, shortly after Ms. Atwood had been named St. Margaret of the Booker, I picked up the phone. The voice on the other end of the line was trembling, like a palsied fawn. "If you put my name in this, I'm dead," she whispered. We agreed that she would be known only as X.

So, how did she like *The Blind Assassin*?

"I didn't like a single character in it," she confessed. "I didn't want to know these people!"

Speaking with X, I felt an overwhelming gush of relief, like a parched summer garden in a cloudburst. I was not alone.

Both of us have witnessed the paeans of praise rising up to honour St. Margaret of the Booker. The endless respectful interviews. The newspaper special supplements. The five-star raves from all over the world. Kakutani loved it. Updike loved it. *The Globe and Mail* loved it. One no-name fellow in some minor local paper did admit that it gave him a headache, but only because it was too brilliant for him. "The publication of a new book by Atwood is greeted with the same awe as a comet . . . streaking by our skies," said one bedazzled bookseller.

Naturally, I ran right out and bought the book. I began to read it, and soon I was suffused with self-doubt. What was wrong with me? I began to feel increasingly uneasy, like a deformed chicken that's about to be pecked to death by the flock. I didn't like the Lizard Men. I didn't like Iris, who, unfortunately, is the main character in the book. I didn't even like Reenie, the lovable housekeeper who has a heart as big as all outdoors and spouts clichés as homey as apple pie and ice cream and as stale as week-old bread. I thought Reenie was tedious beyond belief.

But the wrath of Margaret Atwood is a fearsome thing. One does not want to get on her bad side. I am small, and She is an Icon. She might recognize me one day at Le Select, where we both have lunch sometimes. She might march right up to me and fix me with her pitiless, basilisk eye and strike me dead. Worse, if I cross her, nobody in the Canadian book industry will ever speak to me again.

X doesn't know a single soul in the book industry, but she's scared anyway. "You've got to promise!" she begs. I cross my heart. And she spills her guts.

"I'm a huge fan of hers," she says. "She's a great writer! I took four days off and went to the cottage and this was the only book I took. I know when I buy her books I'm guaranteed an interesting read. And after three hours, I said to my boyfriend, 'Oh, man, this is terrible!'"

X was as wounded as a lover betrayed and as mad as a wet hen. "It was trite and irritating," she says. "It was full of stock characters from central casting. It was sort of like a B-movie."

Sadly, I had to agree with her. No one could be badder than Atwood's villains. You expect them to start twirling their moustaches as they tie ravished virgins to the railway tracks. At first, I thought all this cardboard evil must be ironic, that Ms. Atwood would strike the set and start the real story. But she never did. That *was* the real story.

Aficionados know that, in Atwoodland, a good man is not only hard to find, he's an oxymoron. Men are either weak and spineless or else cruel perpetuators of the patriarchy. Actually, there is one good man in this book, but he's driven into hiding by the wealthy right-wing capitalists, and that makes him cruel, too. (A good capitalist is another oxymoron in Atwoodland.)

Ms. Atwood's schematic view of sexual and class politics might be easier to take if she had a heart. But in all that flipping back and forth among five different narratives, there isn't room for one.

"There's no emotional juice there," wailed Y, another distraught reader who also swore me to secrecy. "It's so cold, so detached. It's like an exercise, not a novel."

To be fair, some people liked this book a lot. Those people included feminist English Lit professors. Here was a gold mine of symbolic material, as rich as a Thanksgiving feast with all the trimmings. Best of all, you don't have to dig too hard for the giblets.

On the planet Zyrcon, for example, men kill, silence and rape, and there are sacrificial virgins who have their tongues cut out to render them speechless. For two points, what parallels can you draw between the planet Zyrcon and the plight of women in mid-twentieth-century Canada? Hint: Our heroine, the one married to the evil Richard, tells us, "My job was to open my legs and shut my mouth."

For five points, you'll also be asked to guess who's the real blind assassin, but I guarantee you'll figure it out.

"I don't know anybody who likes it," confessed Z, who, come to think of it, used to be an English Lit teacher herself. "She's judging all the time, and not with a huge amount of generosity. She's so ironic, so guarded. When has she ever created a character who's genuinely passionate?"

I feel bad setting all this down. Margaret Atwood is a

phenomenally gifted writer. When I discovered *The Edible Woman* nearly three decades ago, I thought it was a revelation. People who write novels for a living deserve to be showered with prizes and parades and riches and honours, and I'm proud that Ms. Atwood's books sell by the millions all over the world, just like hotcakes.

But I'm weary of the brittle puppeteer. And I swear that if I ever again have to read a book with so many ironically inflected clichés or so many forced similes, like palsied fawns staggering across the page, I'm going to ask for my money back.

"It wasn't good enough to put her name on it," said X mournfully.

"We never had this conversation," said Z.

Chapter Two

Early Me

The very first words I ever wrote for *The Globe and Mail* appeared back in 1966, when I was sixteen. I owe this precocious start in journalism to Richard Needham, Canada's most famous curmudgeon. Needham wrote a column for the paper for twenty-three years—a run any columnist would envy—before a callous management hooked him off the stage at the ripe old age of seventy-five. Given his profoundly jaundiced view of human nature, I doubt that he was particularly disappointed. "Knowing what goes on behind my placid exterior, I have a strong suspicion of what goes on behind yours," he once wrote.

Needham delighted in counselling adolescents to misspend their youths. Every Saturday morning he would hold court at the old Lord Simcoe Hotel, where a gang of nerdy teenagers would gather round to drink coffee with him and smoke. He did not believe in convention, and encouraged us to suspect the school system, the well-meaning advice of our parents and institutions of all kinds. We adored him. I was so paralyzed with shyness that I could scarcely say a word to him, but sometimes I would send him something for his column. He used to publish readers' witticisms, and once he solicited suggestions for new and updated song titles in keeping with the times. My immortal debut in print was "Hello, young lovers, you're under arrest."

Needham was an immigrant, like me. The son of an army officer, he came to Canada from England when he was sixteen and claimed that he had worked as a farmhand before showing up at the *Toronto Star,* where he was hired for ten dollars a week. Despite his cranky print persona, he was a kindly man who enjoyed the company of teenage misfits with intellectual pretensions.

One day he offered me a tour of the newspaper. He showed me through the newsroom and introduced me to his assistant, Luscious Lucy (all the women he knew got nicknames like this; he would be considered a hopeless sexist today). The *Globe*'s corridors were lined with famous front pages: the end of World War II, Sputnik, the JFK assassination. Then he took me down to the depths of the composing room, where crusty old men worked the linotype machines with their melting pots of hot lead. The composing room was a dark, rackety, Dickensian place, and I was enchanted. Today the composing room and the crusty men are long gone. But the front pages are still there, and every time I pass them I know that I have the best job in the world.

Needham's irreverence for authority was his most endearing trait. This extended to his own employer, which he renamed *The Mop & Pail, The Groan & Wail, The Grope & Flail,* ad infinitum. As Rudolf J. Needleberry or Rasputin J. Novgorod, he cultivated an alter ego of a faintly disreputable, dirty old man who rescued first-class women from the second-class men who, regrettably, rule the world. When asked what was the one message he wanted remembered out of all his columns, he replied, "That women are far more intelligent than men." But he had our number, too. "Every woman needs one man in her life who is strong and responsible," he once wrote. "Given this security, she can proceed to do what she really wants to do—fall in love with men who are weak and irresponsible."

In person, Needham was neither dirty nor disreputable. He was a tall, crewcut, polite fellow who stayed married to the same wife for fifty-two years. In spite of his loathing for institutions, organized religions and conventional pieties of all kinds, he was a small-c conservative who was deeply suspicious of liberal efforts to reform mankind and perfect the world. It is a prejudice I share to this day.

He once said that his obituary should simply state, "Richard Needham's tiresome and repetitious column will no longer appear because he is dead." He never got his wish, because he was turfed out in 1987, just a few months after I had the miraculous good fortune of being hired by the *Globe* to edit its business magazine. Even I could see that his column had, in truth, outlived its day. He promptly went out and got a job as a foot courier, and never entered the *Globe* building again. From time to time he was spotted with his courier bag in the vicinity of King and Bay, a salutary reminder that no columnist—not even the one who had so much influence on the young me— lasts forever.

My Career as a Smoker

Needham was a chain-smoker. It went along with the hardbitten style of journalists of his era. And I puffed right along with him. Instead of being horrified, he plied me with cigarettes.

I had my first cigarette when I was twelve, on a lovely spring afternoon on a downtown city street. I was playing hooky with my friends Darlene and Sheila. Darlene had a pack of Alpines (a particularly nasty menthol brand with pictures of snow-capped mountains) and gave me one. It tasted absolutely ghastly, but I adored it. It was my first taste of sin.

Taking up smoking is quite difficult because it is so unpleasant. I worked and worked and worked at it. I locked myself into the bathroom and practised for months until I could make smoke come out of my nostrils. I studied this effect from all angles in the mirror, and it was very pleasing. I learned to inhale, and regarded it as the proudest achievement of my fifteenth year.

Was I seduced into smoking by manipulative cigarette advertising? No. Was I hooked on smoking by the addictive effect of nicotine? Emphatically not. I smoked for years before I actually enjoyed the things. I smoked to be worldly. I smoked to be reckless. I smoked to lose weight (it didn't work), and to impress boys. Smoking was an excellent way of being bad, because it wasn't so bad that it would screw up your entire life, like pregnancy or heroin.

My career as a smoker was long and varied. I switched from Alpines to Marlboros, and later to Camels (unfiltered). I even tried Gitanes and Balkan Sobranies because they implied that I had spent a great deal of time on the Left Bank. No low-tar, low-nicotine Virginia Slims for me.

I knew cigarettes corrupted your lungs, fouled your breath and burned holes in your clothes and furniture. But I never imagined I could die from them. Nobody under thirty can imagine dying from anything at all.

And so I have a tip for all those well-meaning Ottawa bureaucrats in the Ministry of Righteousness and Public Virtue and their expensive anti-smoking campaigns. If they truly want to discourage kids from smoking, they ought to hire me as a consultant. Here's my advice.

Ditch the government propaganda. Not so long ago the busy bureaucrats in Ottawa produced an expensive ad depicting young people diving into flaming vats of tar and nicotine. This was supposed to portray the evils of smoking. Any kid could have told them it was about as persuasive as *Reefer Madness*.

Trying to preach virtue to adolescents is a waste of taxpayers' money. Instead, the social engineers should take the contrarian approach. They should, for example, encourage cigarette companies to sponsor wholesome youth activities. Church choirs, Girl Guide troops and Scottish Highland dancing competitions are some possibilities. In other words, turn smoking into something good girls do.

Promote the health benefits. Fill school bulletin boards with posters listing all the ways that cigarettes are good for you.

Make smoking a mandatory part of the school curriculum. That will give it the same appeal as mandatory gym class.

And finally, remember that all the threats, health scares, propaganda and advertising in the universe mean nothing to your average adolescent girl. The only thing that matters is the opinion of her friends.

And so I grew up, hacking happily. Then one day, at the end of the seventies, I visited some friends in trendy San Francisco. After our meal of radicchio and quiche, I lit up in my customary manner. They regarded me with faint distaste, as if I'd scratched my armpits in public. And then I heard, for the first time, the phrase, "This is a non-smoking area."

As I puffed away in exile at the bottom of their garden, I felt the zeitgeist blowing in off the San Francisco Bay. The cultural winds were shifting. Here, in the cradle of all middle-class revolutions, smoking had become an anti-social act. I knew what I had to do.

A year later I quit, cold turkey. It was the proudest achievement of my thirty-first year. Scary government propaganda had nothing to do with my decision. I quit because smoking wasn't sexy anymore, and I was still desperate for approval.

The Pill Changed Everything

When I was in Grade 12, nearly every girl I knew was still a virgin. In other ways, we were no different from eighteen-year-old girls today. All of us were desperate to try out sex. But birth control for teenage girls was still relatively rare, and unwanted pregnancies were a catastrophe.

Have sex, and your life could be ruined before it started. We were horny, but we weren't stupid. We knew where our interests lay.

To my mind, the most revolutionary new technology of our times was not the automobile, the airplane, the microchip, the television or the atom bomb. It was the Pill. Without it, women's liberation never could have happened. The Pill decoupled biology from destiny. In the span of just a generation—my own reproductive lifetime—the Pill has utterly transformed our lives and reshaped society. By one estimate, 80 per cent of North American women born since 1945 have been on the Pill at some time or other.

For a teenage girl today, going on the Pill is just another rite of passage, like going to the prom or applying to go to university. For us, it was secretive and scary.

When I was in Grade 12, selling any type of birth control in Canada was still technically a crime. A loophole in the law made an exception for "the public good," a notion that was conveniently left vague. Contraception was supposed to be available only to married women, so that they could space their children. Young, unmarried women weren't supposed to have it because it might encourage promiscuity. The Pill had only been around for six or seven years, and to get it you had to pretend you had "menstrual disorders." Millions of unmarried women suddenly came down with awful symptoms.

As I dreamed of heading off to university (I would live in a chaperoned women's dorm where sex was theoretically forbidden), I imagined that everybody there must be having sex. It was, after all, 1967, and rumours of the sexual revolution had even reached Toronto. I didn't want my future friends at university to think I was a hick from Don Mills. But I was far too mortified to ask our family doctor for the Pill.

I was even too embarrassed to go to the Hassle Free Clinic (somebody might see me). So I got out the Yellow Pages, chose a doctor's name at random, bought a cheap gold ring at Kresges and told the doctor I was engaged. I was shaking. I thought he might bawl me out or demand to phone my mother.

Instead he wrote me a prescription, which I gratefully took off with me to university. I discovered that rumours of the sexual revolution had been sadly exaggerated, but that's another story.

The Pill meant far more than sex without fear. It meant choice, and not just reproductive choice. It meant that I didn't face the wretched options of my two great-aunts (who chose independent lives, at the cost of being celibate old maids) or my own mother (marriage or med school). It meant that I could be self-sufficient and live my life on more or less equal terms with men. The precipitous decline of marriage—and the rise of divorce—are a direct consequence of the Pill.

Everybody knows about the inventors of the car, the airplane and the atom bomb. Curiously, hardly anyone knows about the inventors of the Pill. It was midwived by two crusading women and a lone-wolf scientist named Gregory Pincus.

One of the women was the birth-control pioneer Margaret Sanger, whose own mother was pregnant eighteen times and dead by the age of forty-one. The other was Katharine Dexter McCormick, a scientifically minded person who was among the first female graduates of MIT and also very rich. It was she who funded Dr. Pincus's research, because no pharmaceutical company would touch it. And it was Dr. Pincus who figured out that the hormone progesterone would suppress ovulation.

Back in the 1950s, most women went to college to get an "MRS" degree. They got married at eighteen or nineteen (as my own mom did) and started having babies right away (three of us by age twenty-six). The Catholic Church was immensely powerful. Priests told women that if they practised birth control they would be haunted forever by the faces of their unborn children.

Instead, doctors gave them vaginal hysterectomies after their third or fourth child. It worked—if they didn't bleed to death.

The Catholic Church was eager to keep the birth rate high and the Catholic population up, especially in Quebec. Elsewhere in Canada, there were fears that if the birth rate fell, immigrants would take over the country and the general IQ would fall. People also feared (rightly, as it turned out) that birth control would lead to widespread sex outside of marriage.

That was only fifty years ago.

Eventually a small drug company, G. D. Searle, agreed to bring the Pill to market—with ten times the hormone levels that it has today. It was approved for use in the United States in 1960, and society changed virtually overnight. The birth rate in Quebec plunged from six or ten or seventeen kids to one or two.

More women became lawyers because law firms no longer had to worry that they might get pregnant in the middle of a case. Women became doctors because they could make sure pregnancies wouldn't interfere with their training. There were no reasons to exclude women from the workplace anymore. We no longer needed an MRS degree. And just as people had feared, we had sex with whomever we wanted.

The Pill decoupled sex and marriage, and it also decoupled marriage and procreation. The purpose of marriage became mutual satisfaction, not children. And once that happened, gay marriage probably became inevitable.

I can still recall how I shook from nerves and shame that day in the doctor's office. I had no idea I was making history. For better and for worse, the West today enjoys a level of personal freedom and autonomy unparalleled in human history—all because women can control their reproductive cycles. The Pill was such a little thing. But the bang it made was bigger than the atom bomb.

A Prof, a Pass and a Co-ed

I went to university during the dawn of the sexual revolution. It was a glorious time on campus. The professors were trading in their ties for love beads. The most popular profs offered courses where you could grade yourself, and fraternized shamelessly with their students. We smoked dope with them. Sometimes we slept with them, or hoped to. Two of my best friends wound up marrying their professors. I spent my last semester futilely trying to seduce my thesis supervisor. In fact, my failure to have a single erotic encounter with a faculty member was a source of great disappointment to me. The Pill had done its work even more quickly than the moralists had feared.

But by 1983, sex on campus was no longer carefree. Every university was obsessed with gender inequity, sexual harassment and power imbalances, and sexual relations had become distinctly problematic. That's when Harold Bloom made the mistake of putting his hand on Naomi Wolf's twenty-year-old thigh at Yale.

Ms. Wolf is a celebrity feminist, best known for a book called *The Beauty Myth*, and also for telling Al Gore how to dress like an alpha male. Harold Bloom, now well into his seventies, is among the most renowned academics in the world, a revered interpreter of Shakespeare and a man of dazzling intellect. According to Ms. Wolf, he's also a dirty old man, whose habit of hitting on attractive female students has been an open secret at Yale. And now she's getting her revenge.

In a long article in *New York* magazine in the spring of '04, she recounted her trauma and accused Yale of letting sexual harassment run unchecked. In 1983, she was a nervous undergraduate who was desperate for him to read her poetry. "He was a vortex of power and intellectual charisma," she wrote. One night he invited himself to dinner at her apartment and guzzled sherry throughout the meal. "You have the aura of election upon you," he breathed, and put his hand up her skirt. She promptly vomited into the kitchen sink from shock, although it's possible the sherry might also have been a factor. "You are a deeply troubled girl," he told her, then corked up his sherry and left. (For the record, Professor Bloom has denied it all.)

The incident, she wrote, "devastated my sense of being valuable to Yale as a student rather than as a pawn of powerful men." But Ms. Wolf (who, it must be noted, is ravishingly beautiful) has received precious little sympathy from the sisterhood, who figure the statute of limitations on this particular gender crime ran out long ago. "It's a desperate power grab," scoffed Katie Roiphe, a well-known feminist who wrote a book on date rape. "People didn't pay attention to her last book on motherhood. She wants to regain the sense of outrage of the feminism of the early 1990s."

"How many times do we have to relive Naomi Wolf's growing up?" fumed the redoubtable Camille Paglia. "Move on! Move on! Get on to the menopause next!"

Although universities don't know it yet, Ms. Wolf's version of victim feminism is as out of date as girdles. Her twenty-year-old effort to get even (and her extravagant claims for the trauma she suffered at the time) strike most people as bizarre. But they're no more bizarre than campus sexual-harassment policies, where victim feminism still reigns supreme. These policies treat every case of boorish, drunken behaviour as sexual predation, and they define sex between faculty and students as essentially illicit. Consensual sex across the lines is deemed to be impossible because of built-in power imbalances.

It's ironic that not so long ago, my friends and I were outraged that university administrations locked us up in women's dorms and insisted on being sex police. We were furious at being treated like helpless children, and insulted that the authorities could regulate our private lives. We could take care of ourselves.

Campus harassment codes have mostly put an end to the days of lecherous professors who preyed on co-eds. But they also perpetuate the myth that sexual advances all go one way. Anyone with any experience of campus life knows otherwise, and any charismatic male professor can tell you how often it's his students who do the chasing. Erotic bonds have sprung up between teachers and pupils since Socrates started giving philosophy lessons in the agora. And they aren't always a bad thing.

Ms. Wolf says she decided to go public after all this time because she owes it to other students, and also because Yale pretty much ignored her phone calls. But I think her real problem with Harold Bloom was that he shattered her illusions. The man she idolized and revered turned out to be a boorish pig. That's another lesson young women have been learning since time immemorial. It's a hard one. But you get over it.

My Life as a Waitress

Every summer in Toronto, when the city gets hot and the humidity presses in, I remember the most formative job I ever had. I've never put it on my résumé, but it was the first job that taught me something about the world. It was also the first job I was ever really good at. Since then I've known that no matter what else happens, I can always make a dollar so long as my legs hold out.

I was a waitress at the Coffee Mill.

It was what I did to make money in the summer during the years I went to college. From May through August, I schlepped espressos and salami sandwiches, oceans of goulash and mountains of pastries and gallons of orange frappés. The accumulated knowledge of five years of higher education has mostly been washed clean from my brain, but thirty years later I can still recite most of the Coffee Mill's menu by heart.

The Coffee Mill was the brainchild of a formidable Hungarian named Martha Rubanyi. She had a husband, but she did all the work. I am forever grateful to her for giving me the job. I came to regard Hungarians as charming and delightful people who are best enjoyed in small amounts, like chestnut purée.

The Coffee Mill offered a hint of continental sophistication in a city that was still hopelessly parochial. The idea that there might exist more than one kind of coffee was still a novelty back then, and ordering an espresso or a cappuccino was a very sophisticated thing to do. Some of the customers were genuine writers, and some were even Europeans. Barbara Amiel came, and one of her early husbands, the Hungarian writer George Jonas, and minor movie actors. In nice weather they could sit outdoors on a terrace, just as the Parisians did. This too was a racy idea in Toronto.

So far as waitressing jobs went, mine was quite high status. I wasn't slinging hash to truckers. I was serving the intelligentsia. I wasn't even required to wear a uniform. I wore a white polyester apron with a miniskirt and high-heeled sandals. Every night I would take the apron home and scrub it with bleach and stitch up the pockets where they had ripped. I kept the tips in there, and by the end of a good shift my apron sagged with quarters. I made ninety-five cents an hour plus tips, and cleared about a hundred bucks a week. I felt rich.

Not many college kids I know have summer jobs like this anymore. They're too busy tutoring inner-city children, or doing research to help find the cure for cancer, or otherwise saving the world and building up their résumés. And that's too bad. A stint of manual labour gives the children of the middle class a first-hand taste of how the other half live. For most of them, it's the only taste they'll ever get.

The other half were waitresses like Ibi. She waitressed for a living, not for the cost of textbooks. She was middle-aged and stout, and she wore those peculiar open-heeled Hungarian-waitress shoes. She ran up and down the stairs to the basement kitchen a hundred times a night, just as I did. We made exactly the same amount of money, except that I probably ended up with more because I was nineteen and wore a miniskirt. I felt vaguely guilty about this natural advantage. I knew that long after I moved on, she would be running up and down those stairs until her legs gave out.

I wonder if she resented the fresh young college girls who came to work there in the summer. I know I would have.

I became an excellent waitress, if I do say so myself. I liked the physicality and the flow of it. At its best it was like a news-paper at deadline time, when the work builds and builds until all hell breaks loose and a million things are going on at once, and then it's finished and you all go home. I could keep com-plicated orders in my head and carry four plates in my left hand. I could add a bill up fast and make the change and never get it wrong (no calculators, then). At night I would sleep the sleep of the physically exhausted, an experience I would rarely have again.

There is an order and proficiency to good waitressing that only other waitresses can truly appreciate. There is also a valuable opportunity to observe the vagaries of human nature from lower down in the pecking order. You quickly learn that rich people can be rude and stingy, and poor people can be courteous and generous, and famous people run the gamut from horrible to very nice. If you really want to know the truth about someone's character, talk to the people who serve him. If people interviewed the secretaries of executives before they hired them, they would avoid many stupid hiring mistakes. But they never do.

Of course I was sexually harassed. Find me somebody who wasn't. That was a valuable life lesson too. There was no term for it back then, and you were on your own. The married middle-aged manager enjoyed what I thought to be a harmless flirtation with most of the young waitresses, including me. Gradually it became a bit less harmless. One day he invited me up to his apartment and, like an idiot, I went. He made a pass, I fled in horror and he never flirted with me again. I wondered if he'd try to get back at me, but he didn't.

The Coffee Mill carries on, although I hardly ever go there anymore. It feels a bit like visiting my old high school, where I'm still intimidated by the French teacher. I know it's ridiculous, but I can't help it. Martha still presides and, like the menu, has scarcely changed. I hope that she remembers me with fondness. Through the years, the thought that I've acquired an honest trade has often reassured me. If all else fails, I tell myself, I can always go back to waitressing.

Heartthrobs

To this day I can scarcely quote a line of Shakespeare, but the first paragraph of *Gone with the Wind* is engraved forever on my heart. Between the time I was ten and the time I was seventeen, I read *Gone with the Wind* twenty-two times completely through. Some years, I would get to page 689, where Scarlett O'Hara says, "After all, tomorrow is another day," and turn straight back to page 1 and that immortal opening: "Scarlett O'Hara was not beautiful, but men seldom realized it when caught by her charm as the Tarleton twins were."

My favourite edition of the book was the paperback with the picture on the cover of Scarlett swooning in Rhett Butler's arms. I wore out at least three copies. I would read it until the spine cracked and the glue fell off and the pages shredded all over my bedroom. Even at age ten, I knew that picture had something to do with male magnetism, though I was hazy about the details, and I looked forward to the day when *I* would swoon in someone's arms. Even then I suspected I would never have a seventeen-inch waist and eyes starred with bristly lashes, but I figured I could fake it.

All through Grade 7 my best friend, Jane, would come over and we would spend delicious hours together reading our favourite passages to each other. (" 'Sir,' she said, 'you are no gentleman!' 'An apt observation,' he answered airily. 'And you, Miss, are no lady.' ") These especially included the kissing scenes.

But it wasn't until I was twelve or so that I discovered that *Gone with the Wind* was actually the hottest book in the English language. There is a terrific scene on the porch in Atlanta where Rhett asks Scarlett to be his mistress. The significance of this scene had always eluded me, and I tended to skip over it since it didn't have any kissing. "Mistress" was one of those words I hadn't figured out yet, like "reconstruction." But one day I realized the steamy truth. "Mistress" didn't mean mistress. It meant—*mistress!* More was going on here than met the eye.

I was astonished that Margaret Mitchell had been allowed to put something like that in a book that children might read. I hoped that my mother hadn't read it, too. And slowly it occurred to me that there might be other things going on between Scarlett and Rhett than kissing. With heart racing madly, I searched out page 625, the swooning scene, where Rhett sweeps Scarlett off her feet and carries her up the stairs into the swirling darkness.

After the swirling darkness comes a double space (or three asterisks, depending on which edition you have), and then it's the next morning. No doubt about it. Something sexy had been going on in that white space.

It has been thirty years since I last read *Gone with the Wind*. Yet no matter how often I tell myself that what counts in a man is honesty, responsibility and being kind to small animals, when I level with myself, I know it's not true. What counts is dialogue like "You've had this coming to you for years. None of the fools you've known have kissed you like this—have they?" What counts is breath that burns through the taffeta against your skin. What counts is slow, hot lips, and someone who can kiss like Rhett Butler.

My Grade 11 English teacher, who had hair down to her waist and had been married twice, was not impressed when I told her my favourite author was Margaret Mitchell. With one suggestion, she supplanted Rhett Butler in my fantasy life and upgraded my taste in literature. She told me to read Leonard Cohen.

Leonard Cohen was the first poet I ever read who was not only still alive, but certifiably Canadian, and—I could scarcely believe what I was reading—hot. At the time, he was not part of the approved curriculum. The educational authorities thought he was a dirty-minded beatnik.

Until then, I thought poetry was a chore, like physics. Once I discovered it was subversive, I embraced it with the full force of my sublimated teenage lust. I cranked out doom-laden verse by the yard. And I only hoped that Leonard Cohen would wait for me to reach the age of majority, so that I could make it up to him for Suzanne.

At university, I majored in subversive poets and fell in love with brooding assistant English professors who looked like Leonard Cohen. (I thought it must be the meaninglessness of the universe that made them so glum, when actually they were worrying about getting tenure.) Afterward, I hitchhiked all through Europe, getting drunk on the glory that was Rome and hoping to run into Leonard Cohen, who was rumoured to hang out there.

When I finished university, I had two aims in life: to meet poets and to earn a living. This conjunction of literary idealism and stark necessity has for centuries provided the book publishing industry with a steady stream of cheap labour. As I sat in the basement of the book publisher's office carrying out my first assignment, which was to put five thousand backlist titles in alphabetical order, I imagined Leonard Cohen in brooding exile on his Greek island. I suspected he was having more fun than I was.

Eventually I was promoted upstairs and got to meet real authors. Some of them were even poets. Alas for me, none of them resembled Leonard Cohen in the least. Instead of seducing women and finding the meaning of life, they whined about their royalties, the cover designs on their books and their rotten reviews. Instead of muses, they had mortgages, wives and screaming babies. And they were lousy dressers.

On the whole, great poets are smart to die young. Their tragic early demise cements their reputation. A long life tends to turn poets into desperately dull and solid citizens, like Wordsworth, or ridiculous old swains, like Irving Layton.

But Leonard Cohen's charm has defied age. In fact, he has turned it to his advantage. "My friends are gone and my hair is grey," he sings in that devastating whisky voice, "and I ache in the places where I used to play." No one has ever made decrepitude sound more attractive. Besides, he knows that we know that mere stamina means nothing.

Joan Crate is a professor of English at Red Deer College in Alberta, a long-time scholar of Coheniana and, like me, a helpless fan. Leonard Cohen, she believes, is a fatal combination of Heathcliff and Byron. "He's a modern romantic hero. He's mysterious, so you get to fill in the blanks. He behaves badly, so women feel they can reform him." Best of all, he's in such torment. Every woman secretly knows she could help him work on that.

Not surprisingly, certain men have a little trouble with Leonard Cohen. Here's a guy who smoked too much, drank too much, fooled around too much and seems to have evaded all family responsibilities. When other guys were taking out a twenty-five-year mortgage, he took a twenty-five-year-old to Greece.

And what happened to him? His voice got better. His songs got better. He made hit albums. At an age when other guys were wondering whether they needed more life insurance, he was on MTV. He published a best-selling book—of poetry. He ran around with gorgeous movie stars, until he got tired of them and went to live in a monastery with his Zen master. There he scrubs floors and ponders the meaning of existence.

No wonder there's a hostile little undercurrent to the coverage he's received. One journalist called him a "durable hipster" and then told us that his sagging jowls have "added a touch of Golda Meir" to his looks. Someone else called him the bard of the bedsits. "A ravaged roué," wrote another, who went on to wonder whether he was "a poseur or a prophet," or perhaps just a Barry Manilow for people with B.A.'s.

And, let's face it, even his female admirers have a couple of problems with Leonard. Does he have to run through those muses quite so fast? Do they have to be quite so young? Why do they stay the same age while the rest of us get older?

Professor Crate knows that she and I don't stand a chance with Leonard. Maybe it's just as well. She's old enough to know what really happens when you let a poet in the house. At a Leonard Cohen symposium, she once delivered a witty account of life with Leonard, told from the muse's point of view, just after the romantic moment is over. "We all know what happens next," she said. "The poet-lover deflates, and writes a poem. Woman brushes her teeth, makes supper, does the laundry." And you can bet that no one writes a poem about it.

Leonard Cohen's life and work would never survive a feminist critique. So how is it possible to be both a feminist and a lifelong Cohen fan? Fortunately, his fans aren't interested in consistency.

I discovered him at the same time as I discovered all of life's other great verities—art, love and vague but powerful spiritual yearnings. Most of the time it was hard to tell which was which, but Leonard's poetry gave legitimacy to them all. I left behind my old Beatles albums many, many moves ago. But I never left behind my copy of *The Spice Box of Earth*.

The Shoulder-Pad Decade

Long before *Sex in the City*, there was Toronto in the eighties. It was a city full of young career women striving to make their way in a world their mothers would scarcely recognize. I was one of them. We were determined to be independent. We were determined to combine feminism with femininity and motherhood with work. We were competing with men, and also falling in love and getting married to them. My girlfriends and I all wanted babies—but later, after we found the right (liberated but also successful) husband, the dream house, the perfect job. For some of us, later never came.

As a child of divorce, I wasn't in a big rush to get married. This was just as well, because in those days I had an unerring instinct for Mr. Wrong. There was a whole string of them.

There was the Nordic god who liked to cycle up mountains, run marathons and canoe great rivers. He got huffy when I couldn't keep up. "Why are you so out of shape?" he would say. There was the man who lived in Australia, and the one who lived in Rome. There was, naturally, the married one, who tore my heart out and stomped all over it until it was just a grease stain on the road. It took me several thousand dollars worth of expensive therapy to realize that our star-crossed relationship was just another pathetic cliché.

By that time I had bought a house, since it was obvious that no one was about to buy one for me. My mom helped me with the down payment. The house was in the Beaches, an artistic section of Toronto where everyone voted NDP and either worked for the CBC or practised some kind of holistic therapy. I bought it from a couple who were splitting up. The wife was an art photographer who took pictures of nude men in the woods, which corporations paid her thousands of dollars for. One night, before the deal closed, I took over a bottle of wine to celebrate with her. I'll never forget her words of wine-soaked wisdom. "Men come and men go," she said, "but art and real estate are forever."

In the eighties I worked as the editor of a couple of well-known business magazines, chronicling the triumphs and follies of tycoons and the progress of women in the workplace. Like all working women, I had a closet full of jackets with monster shoulder pads. Everything came with shoulder pads, even underwear. They look ridiculous now, but back then they made perfect sense. Subconsciously we believed that if we dressed like linebackers, maybe it would be easier to crash though those glass ceilings.

Everything we wore was oversized. We had giant glasses that covered half our faces. We had severe maxi-skirts that went halfway down our calves, and blouses that buttoned high around our necks. Our business suits were black or brown or pinstriped, like men's suits, and some of us wore little pseudo-ties around our necks. No skin showed. In winter we covered ourselves with poufy down coats that made us look like the Michelin Woman. Thus armoured, we stormed the barricades of banks, law firms, newspaper offices and other places men ruled. We wore these clothes for the same reason cats fluff themselves up when they meet a bigger cat. They had a message: "Don't mess with us."

The eighties was the Power Decade, so we wore power suits. We had power lunches at glitzy Toronto restaurants like Fenton's and the Courtyard Café. But secretly, underneath our armour, we longed to be swept away by some investment banker who kissed like Rhett and wrote poetry like Leonard.

For a brief time in the eighties I wrote a column for the *Toronto Star*. It was meant to be a chronicle of the ups and downs of single life, and it tackled such pressing social issues as when you should take your toothbrush on a date. Unknown to me, its readers included my future husband. After we met, he confessed that he had read it, and that even then, he liked the person who wrote it.

At the beginning of the sexual revolution, Gloria Steinem declared that a woman without a man was like a fish without a bicycle. We adored her for this, and we congratulated ourselves for escaping our mothers' fate of getting married at age eighteen and turning into mad suburban housewives. As life went on, we began to think that having a bicycle might be rather nice. But as we discovered, a good one was hard to find.

Around the middle of the decade, a social panic struck regarding the plight of the single woman. The story spread that if you were a single woman over thirty-five, the odds of getting married were about the same as being hit by lightning. This was baloney but we all believed it. To us, the future looked particularly bleak. My girlfriends and I joked that we'd given up on holding out for Mr. Right. We'd settle for Mr. Right Now, so long as he was more or less single, solvent and straight.

The world was full of men who wanted to have sex with us. That wasn't the problem. The problem was a little detail we called the "C-word"—commitment. Men were phobic about it. Clearly some things never change. What would the writers of *Sex and the City* have done without C-phobia as a plot device? But long before Mr. Big came along, I was writing about the C-word and, without knowing it, describing how I met my husband. Here's a piece I wrote in 1986, the year I met him.

Men and the Big C

Between every man and every woman who are somewhere between the first date and the altar, there falls a shadow. I call it the Big C. It is easier to refer to it by its first initial, because the real name is too scary to say out loud in front of anyone with XY chromosomes. Of course, I'm talking about c*mm*tm*nt.

Every woman knows that when it comes to discussing the

Big C, most Canadian men would rather be dead. They can talk openly of their passion for the Detroit Tigers or their love for their BMW. But mention the Big C and watch them flee. Just see what happens the next time you fix him his favourite garlic chicken with a nice bottle of Remy Pannier to wash it down and then try to slip it in. "Say," you say casually, "I wonder if we could talk about you and me and our, you know, c*mm*tm*nt."

There are four standard responses to this ploy. The first is to pretend he misheard the question. "The guy at the body shop said he could hammer out the dent," he might answer. Or, "I think the Liberals are in trouble."

The second response is to act as if you'd tried to choke him on the chicken bones. "Well," he says belligerently, "if you don't know how I feel by now, then I certainly don't know what else I can do to convince you."

Then there are the ones who can't manage any response at all. Instead, their bodies go rigid as they search out the nearest exit. Many small mammals actually suffer cardiac arrest under such stress. This terror is absolutely authentic. But it is also an effective method of persuading you never, ever to ask a question like that again.

Occasionally you may be involved with an exceptionally expressive man. When you bring up the Big C with this type, he lets out a strangulated little gurgle and then admits, "Well, gosh, I guess I like you pretty much." In Canada, this is worth at least ten sonnets by Shakespeare.

Even if you think you have this kind of man, though, you should probably avoid mentioning anything about the Big C at all until you have lived together for at least three years and you're carrying his first child under your heart.

Once you get used to men's ways, you may be able to detect the signs of commitment without having to ask. One important sign is if his name is on the mortgage next to yours. Another sign is if he has stopped referring to the cat as "it," or as "your" cat, as in "Your cat threw up on the rug again."

An almost certain sign is if you've bought a house together and he has actually unpacked his CD collection and mixed it up with yours. (Some men I know have been married for a decade and still keep their CDs filed separately, in case they want to make a fast, clean getaway.)

These signs may not be perfect, but I have come to understand them. So imagine my surprise when I began going out with a man who seemed willing to discuss this forbidden subject. On the first date he said, "I'm really having a good time." Normally, any man who says this to you is married. But this man fooled me by turning out to be single.

On the second date he revealed an intimate secret about himself. I thought that was the last I'd see of him for sure. Normally, any man who reveals an intimate secret gets so embarrassed that he never calls you again. But this man fooled me by calling again.

On the third date he said, "I really do like you a lot, and I hope we get to be good friends, and what are you doing for the next twenty-eight Saturday nights?"

I couldn't believe my ears. I thought it might be some kind of scam. I thought that maybe I should slam the door in his face and change my phone number the next day. I was so frightened that I started searching for the nearest exit. Instead I told myself to breathe deeply, and slowly my panic subsided.

Eventually we moved in together and mixed up our CDs. Although he was a darn good kisser, he looked nothing like Rhett Butler. He never has carried me up the stairs. But he passed the test of the three S's—single, solvent and straight—and then some. Lightning had struck.

Chapter Three

Confessions of a Mid-Life Bride

Although they are a proud and hot-blooded race, the Scots are also nothing if not prudent. They are careful with their money, and they take their time making up their minds. Probably that's why it took my husband and me eleven years to get married. He is a McLeod and I am a McNeill on my mother's side, and we approached matrimony with the speed of mating turtles. Even after I moved into his house, I kept my own house, just in case. You never know when you might want it back.

Six years later, we went to France. His parents were celebrating their fiftieth wedding anniversary and had invited us to share a vacation in Provence with them. One evening the two of us went off for a quiet dinner by ourselves in a small medieval town that looked too quaint to be real. It was the finest meal we'd ever had. Over the dessert and digestifs and the staggeringly large bill, he fell to the old stone floor on one knee and tenderly begged for my hand. Although we'd known each other for only a decade, I cast prudence to the winds and tearfully said yes. I figured that if I played my cards right I could persuade him to come back to France on our honeymoon and keep on eating.

Outside, in the deserted town square, we embraced in the moonlight as the old clock on the town hall struck midnight. It was grand. Nothing could have been more romantic. I was going to be a bride at last. How wonderful. How marvellous. How terrifying.

And so we set the date. And to my horror, I soon found myself as obsessed with wedding trivia as any twenty-two-year-old. What kind of invitations should we choose? What should they say? What kind of typeface would best express our deep commitment to each other? But all these weighty matters paled beside the big one: the wedding dress.

What becomes an aging bride on her trip to the altar? Nothing, I found, that the wedding industry has to offer. Clouds of tulle look ludicrous on someone of mature years. The wedding industry really offers only two dress options: Beautifully Bridal Barbie (not fit for anyone over thirty) and Mother Of (not fit for anyone). If you are over thirty, skip the bridal salons. You're on your own.

It was easy to figure out what I wanted in a wedding outfit. It needed to be elegant, comfortable and recyclable. Aging brides are nothing if not pragmatic. It also needed to make me look tall and narrow instead of short and squat. (I was born to pull a plow.) The hard part was where to find it. I had visions of dragging myself, dazed and confused, through every women's clothing store in Toronto. I hadn't even started to shop and already I was depressed.

Bridegrooms have it easy. All they need to do is drop in at a menswear shop and pick up a basic black designer suit. Total time invested: thirty minutes. Total self-esteem invested: zero. They've laid nothing on the line but their credit card, and they will not be judged. Brides are in a different boat. We'll be judged on style, taste, originality, hairdo, muscle tone and general dress sense. No wonder we get performance anxiety.

And then I thought of Nina.

Nina had a dress store in Yorkville. She made clothes that would make a hippopotamus look sexy. Maybe if I begged her she would make my wedding dress.

When I went to beg her, Nina's eyes lit up. "Oh, a weed-ing!" she breathed, and clasped her hands in joy. Nina was a six-foot-tall French-Russian who spoke English with a ravishing but barely comprehensible accent. She told me breathlessly about some fabric she had last year that would be perfect for a weeding suit; she was out of it, but she might be able to get some more. At least that's what I think she said.

The next week Nina and I inspected a metre of creamy linen. Nina sketched an outfit on a little piece of paper. The skirt was long and tulipy. The jacket had long, narrow sleeves and a high, rounded collar that reminded me of Snow White. "I want to look tall and narrow," I said. Nina promised that I would.

Then I was measured by Nina's Greek seamstress, Kathy. Kathy announced with joy that I was perfectly proportioned.

Regrettably, each proportion has expanded since I was twenty-two. Kathy told Nina that the suit must be cut in size 12. This was disappointing, since in other stores I am a size 10. This is because other stores lie and Kathy tells the truth.

At the first fitting, the skirt fit perfectly and Kathy and Nina argued over whether to put the top button on my jacket a centimetre higher or lower. Kathy did not like my bra. "It makes your bosom go poufy," she told me.

At the second fitting they had another argument about the buttons, and Kathy nipped in the jacket by a centimetre. This time I made sure my bosom wasn't going poufy.

At the third fitting, the buttons were fine. The bosom was fine. But not the jacket. "You lost weight," frowned Kathy. "I can tell." Sure enough, prenuptial nerves had shrivelled me to size 11½. The jacket needed altering by one last millimetre. "Is necessary," Nina breathed. "Will make big difference."

The next day I returned to pick up the finished product. Nina removed two invisible threads and packed my outfit lovingly in tissue paper. Kathy gave me a hug. Nina wished me a happy weeding.

It didn't seem right to get married at City Hall, so we got married in our backyard. To my everlasting shame, I almost missed the wedding.

All our families had gathered from far and near. All our friends had come too. The minister (we've always called her "the minister who will marry anybody") was waiting, resplendent in a multicoloured robe of no particular denomination. The photographer was poised for action. The wedding cake was ready to be cut, the champagne chilling. Just one thing was missing. Me.

I was upstairs, in the bathroom, trying to decide which colour of lipstick to put on.

In real life I am the most practical and down-to-earth of women, good in an emergency, invariably calm and collected. I had made the wedding plans with no conniption fits and no second thoughts at all. It wasn't that I'd got cold feet. It was that my feet had turned into cement. I couldn't move them. I couldn't move anything.

When it became clear that I was stuck, my future husband came up from the garden and poked his head into the bathroom. "Just came up to see how you're doing," he said affably. He used the same calm and reassuring tone of voice that you would use to talk someone out of jumping off a window ledge.

"Wear this one," said my friend Wendy, who was hovering helpfully nearby, and handed me a lipstick.

After I put the lipstick on, I went into the bedroom and sat down on the bed. I sat there for quite a while, sobbing. Then my baby sister came upstairs to see me. She was a social worker who specialized in counselling emotionally disturbed and suicidal teenagers. Somebody had told her that professional intervention was required. She took my hand and spoke soothingly to me until I stopped sobbing. Gently, as if I were an invalid, she led me downstairs to the garden. I clutched my bouquet of white roses with one hand and gripped my poor groom with the other. "Don't let go of me," I muttered, "or I'll fall down." And he didn't. And that's how we got married.

And that's why we've been married ever since.

Psst! Married Is Better

Not long before my wedding, a woman I admired faxed me a sentimental poem. She'd been married for more than thirty years, and the poem was called "Married Is Better." I was shocked. I hid it away so that my single friends wouldn't see it.

Until I got married, I believed in Gloria Steinem's "fish without a bicycle" maxim with all my heart. I knew what the research said. Married women are miserable. Married men are happy. Single women are happier than married ones, and single men are unhappier than married ones but not as unhappy as married women, who are stressed, oppressed and depressed. Marriage is a lopsided affair—good for them, bad for us.

Fortunately, the research is baloney.

The truth is that marriage is good for everyone—men and women, gay and straight, young and old. Humans are happiest when they're pair-bonded.

Married people are generally more contented and live longer than single people or even those who live common-law. They have higher incomes and lower unemployment levels. Marriage encourages stability, responsibility and continuity. It teaches you the virtues of tolerance, temperance, forbearance, respect and mutual obligation. Besides, spouses are useful. Who else is going to help you find your reading glasses?

The benefits of marriage for gay couples are the same as for everybody else. They settle down and become responsible. They buy real estate. They cut their grass and improve their property values. I'm amazed that we regard gay marriage as a radical idea. In fact, nothing could be more conservative, boring and bourgeois.

The marital unit is the bedrock of middle-class society, and a flourishing middle class is the greatest guarantor ever known of peace, order and good government. Getting married is just about the most Canadian thing somebody can do. Married couples save and invest. They buy RRSPs, renovate their kitchens, faithfully pay their income tax and separate their garbage. They look after each other in sickness and old age, so that the state doesn't have to.

Marriage, in short, is such a beneficial instrument of public policy that the state ought to provide large incentives to everyone to take the plunge. If the Christian right, REAL Women and Focus on the Family genuinely believed in family values, they'd be first in line to demand marriage licences for gay and lesbian couples, and would show up to throw the rice.

To my surprise, not all gay men and women believe in marriage. Some call themselves anti-assimilationists. They want the state to stay out of their bedrooms, and also out of their financial arrangements. They have no desire to play by the straight world's rules. They want to make their own rules. They want to reject traditional institutions, not reinvent them.

I once felt exactly the same way. I thought people should unite as free spirits—no obligation, so long as it was groovy. Marriage was a ball and chain, and it struck me as representing a total failure of imagination. As it turned out, I discovered that this idealistic concept of equal and unencumbered relationships worked much better for some people (men) than for others (women). Nor did it contemplate a time when free spirits would acquire houses, mutual funds, children, a twelve-piece set of bone china and other encumbrances.

So marriage is good for men, children, same-sex couples

and society. And anyone who says it's bad for women is not acquainted with the facts.

"The evidence is mountainous in the other direction," says sociology professor Linda Waite. "Marriage makes women significantly happier."

Linda Waite is the (happily married) co-author of a book called *The Case for Marriage*. She's set out to show that married women lead longer, happier, healthier, less depressed, more affluent lives than single women do. They even have better (and more) sex. Just like married men. "Married women are mentally and emotionally healthier than single women," she told me.

"Getting married actually boosts your happiness. For example, it means you're a lot less lonely."

I reflected on my single life and realized she was right. I remember all those years I spent eating my nicely cooked little suppers all by myself. (No Kraft Dinner for me. That was for pathetic-loser single guys.) Even when life was dreary and miserable, I kept trying to persuade myself that I was a lot better off than most wives. I felt sorry for them. I also secretly wanted to be one.

I used to think it was weak of me to want to be married. I thought that if I felt lonely it was my fault. "Actually, being lonely is one of the best reasons to get married," Dr. Waite told me. "Married people always have someone to talk to who cares about them."

This is true. Even if the someone you're talking to is actually thinking about the hockey playoffs.

But what's the point of getting married if you already live

together, apart from the great excuse to go on a honeymoon and eat your way through France?

"You'll be richer," she says. "Getting a lifelong, permanent economic partner makes you much better off financially in a variety of ways. Our research shows that married people nearing retirement have assets nearly twice as high as single people. Two people who are just living together are far less likely to share their money." Or, for that matter, to take turns cleaning out the litter box.

Yet surely, I argued, being trapped in a lousy, rotten marriage is worse than getting a divorce.

"Not necessarily. Most couples who say they are quite unhappy with their marriage but stay married are much happier five years later. Good marriages can go bad. But bad marriages quite often go good."

I thought of all the married couples I know who were miserable when their kids were little and they were broke and tired. I thought of the best friend who used to come over and throw herself on my couch and vow to leave her husband and run away to France. She never did. Now the kids are grown, the mortgage is paid off and she and the husband she couldn't stand for one more second are devoted to each other. They had a good marriage that went bad and then went good. They just had to wait it out.

Until I talked to Dr. Waite, I thought I must be one of the lucky few who had managed to beat the odds on marital misery for wives. But it turns out that most wives aren't miserable at all. Although I'd never tell this to my single women friends, married life beats single life roughly seven days out of seven.

My married girlfriends and I speak about this fact from time to time among ourselves. We always sound a little surprised and a little guilty about our happiness. After all, we do not wish to break the ranks of female solidarity or take the risk of sounding old-fashioned or judgmental. We all recall the bad old days when people looked down on single women. We all feel that it's as rude to say "married is better" in mixed company as it is to say that two legs are better than one, or thin is more attractive than fat.

But it's true. Please don't tell.

Chapter Four

I Was Conrad Black's Boss

Sometime in 1987, Conrad Black's secretary phoned to invite me to a private luncheon at Ten Toronto Street, the elegant downtown building which was, at that time, still the capital of his business empire. I was flattered and also curious, because I had not yet met him even though I was his boss.

Yes, I was Conrad's boss. He wrote a monthly column for the magazine I edited, and we paid him handsomely for it.

The fact that Mr. Black did not own the magazine (*The Globe and Mail* did) contributed mightily to his pride in writing for it. His monthly cheque was proof that he had standing as a paid journalist, a profession for which he has from time to time expressed great contempt. Privately, Mr. Black has always selectively admired journalists (he married one, after all), and what drove him to write his column is what drives us all: being a columnist gives you a giddy, misplaced sense of power and influence. If you can't be a lord, as Mr. Black later became, being a columnist is the next best way to show off.

As I set off for Ten Toronto, I wondered why Conrad Black wanted to lunch with me. Perhaps it was to discuss his recent acquisition of *The Telegraph* or to bounce around a few column ideas. None of my other columnists had a private dining room with a chef, so I was also looking forward to a splendid meal.

Lunch began with a stupefying blast of erudition from my host. Conversation is the wrong word, since Mr. Black did all the talking. I remember very little of what he said, though I do recall that both Pitt the Elder and Pitt the Younger made an appearance. The cumulative effect of this monologue was to make me feel like the most stupid person on earth, a sensation I later learned I shared with most people who encountered Mr. Black for the first time. Margaret Thatcher, a lady who could hold her own with anyone, once confessed she'd felt exactly the same way.

The verbal barrage, it turned out, was merely a tactic to weaken my mental faculties and prepare the ground for a full frontal assault. After forty-five minutes or so, Mr. Black got round to the real reason for the lunch. He wanted a raise.

As I feebly tried to point out to him, Mr. Black was not at that time underpaid. Quite the contrary. He had managed to extort the astonishing sum of $1,200 per column from my predecessor, a person whose spine was even weaker than my own. That made him perhaps the highest-paid magazine columnist in Canadian journalism, next to Allan Fotheringham.

At the mention of Allan Fotheringham, Mr. Black drew himself up to his full height. Did I mean to tell him that another magazine columnist made more money than he did? How much more? What were his readership numbers, compared to Mr. Black's? How could this discrepancy in compensation be justified? For the next twenty minutes, he grilled me on who made what, and why. Never mind that Mr. Black did not, in fact, make his living from writing, or that the cheques he got from us were less than a rounding error in his bank account. The money was not the point. Mr. Black could not be happy unless he was certain he was top of the heap.

This hypercompetitive reflex is common in successful men. They are, after all, great apes, and status-seeking is hard-wired into their brains. Canada's small elite of extremely rich businessmen are all finely tuned to the precise status (i.e., net worth) of their rivals. Among the hypersuccessful, the competition extends to all areas of conspicuous consumption. Who has the biggest house? The best private island? The most impressive jet? The loveliest and most accomplished wife? They keep close track of those things.

Then there are the equally important intangibles of prestige and reputation. Peter Munk got Brian Mulroney for his board. But Conrad Black got Margaret Thatcher and George Bush Sr. for his. Peter Munk donated $5 million to the Toronto Hospital to build a state-of-the-art cardiac centre with his name on it. Very soon after that, Conrad Black donated $5 million to the Hospital for Sick Children. Until recently, Conrad Black rode around town in a chauffeured limousine, but Peter Munk rides around town in a taxi and once told me he thought Mr. Black's limousine was ridiculously pretentious.

In the end, the lunch with Mr. Black did not go well. The food was in the finest British tradition, which is to say, plain, overdone and tasteless. The wine was Canadian, and cheap. But I paid dearly. By the time the coffee came he had extorted a raise of $150 a month, which was shamefully more than the measly increase that *Globe and Mail* reporters got that year. I never lived it down.

If Conrad Black had decided to be a full-time writer instead of a tycoon, life probably would have worked out pretty well for him. "I think it is more personally rewarding to him to be a significant literary person," his former friend Hal Jackman told me. But writers don't have jets and Palm Beach mansions, and Mr. Black had a craving for those status markers at whatever cost. It's those alpha genes that drive men like him to the top, and it's the alpha genes that bring them down.

Why I'll Never Be CEO

I worked for eleven years as a business editor at *The Globe and Mail*, first at *Report on Business Magazine* and later at the daily business section. These jobs gave me a close-up look at the triumphs and follies of capitalism and capitalists, most of whom are still male. It was pretty much the same at my own company. At some management meetings I was the only woman in the room. Up the org chart until you reached head office far, far away, there was not a single woman to be seen. Men ruled. Working in management sometimes reminded me of the time in Grade 3 when I decided to crash through the gender barrier on the schoolbus and claim my right to sit in the boys' section. I won, but it wasn't all that much fun in the end.

The day I realized I wasn't cut out to climb the corporate ladder was the day the publisher (a former soup-company executive) burst into my cubicle in the midst of some corporate crisis. He was there to demand urgent action. To make sure I got the point, he pounded his fist on my desk and declared, "Our balls are on the line here!"

That was when I knew I just didn't have the equipment for the job.

"Speak for yourself," I muttered, after he had left the room. But as time passed and I observed the goings-on in corporate life, it became increasingly clear to me that the absence of these objects made it exceedingly unlikely that I would ever become captain of a big enterprise, with a captain's pay, perks, stock options, pension plan and amazing severance package when they finally made me walk the plank, which is the customary fate of captains of industry.

Many people blame systemic discrimination for the absence of women at the top of corporate life. They have a point. But I think there's another factor that's far more elemental: testosterone. Testosterone is the irreducible dividing line between the sexes, the hormone we don't like to mention because we want to believe that all playing fields can be levelled. And it's testosterone that fuels the drive to power.

This conclusion makes me cranky. But it's the only way to account for the fact that, a generation after liberation, hardly any women run big businesses. Despite our equal, if not superior, brains and talent, we make up a vanishingly small percentage of the top dogs on life's greasy pole. A lot of those dogs aren't that smart. But they've got more T (and I mean this in the literal sense) than anyone else in the room.

The case for the pervasive social effects of T, and the persistence of male dominance, was laid out in distressing detail by the writer Andrew Sullivan. Mr. Sullivan is not just a student of T, but a customer. He shoots himself up with synthetic T to offset the debilitating effects of HIV, and thus is able to deliver a first-hand account of what it does to him.

"I can actually feel its power on a daily basis," he wrote. "I feel a deep surge of energy . . . My attention span shortens. In the two or three days after my shot, I find it harder to concentrate on writing and feel the need to exercise more. My wit is quicker, my mind faster, but my judgment is more impulsive . . . In a word, I feel braced. For what? It scarcely seems to matter."

Women have testosterone, too. But men have anywhere from five to twenty-five times more of it. Even men with very low T have much, much more of it than any woman.

When it comes to who's on top, T will probably trump society's best efforts to open the gates of power to all. It is what explains why you don't find very many women who are day traders or race-car drivers, trial lawyers, tycoons or boxers. Women do not shine in lines of work that reward brutal aggressiveness and a taste for blood. They're more likely to shine as university presidents. Of course, not many men lust to beat up other people either. But at the very end of the bell curve of aggressive human behaviour, you will find one sex only. And it's not mine.

It's no accident that the prevailing metaphors of business are borrowed from the battlefield. Your competition is the enemy, and your job is to grind them to dust. Takeovers are battles. Marketing is warfare. This language was not invented by journalists to brighten up dull business copy. It's the way men naturally talk and think.

"You gotta draw blood to win," says a newspaper advertisement for a conference entitled Retail on the Cutting Edge. "You need a battle plan to thrive."

To make the world more civilized, we try to make men less bloodthirsty, not women more so. This is a good thing (except when we punish little boys for not being more like girls). But the will to dominance doesn't go away. It just gets channelled into building mighty business enterprises and scheming how to squash the competition like a bug. Bill Gates is no jock, but make no mistake, he's got Big T.

"The Big T correlates with energy, self-confidence, competitiveness, tenacity, strength and sexual drive," Mr. Sullivan writes. "A forty-year-old executive who took testosterone for body-building purposes told me, 'I walk into a business meeting now and I just exude self-confidence. I know there are lots of other reasons for this, but my company has just exploded since my treatment. I'm on a roll. I feel capable of almost anything.'"

There are large downsides to T. It's what keeps the jails full of young men (not women). It explains our ridiculous retirement age of sixty-five (enterprises need to shed old men with waning T and replace them with young guys who are full of it). And the combination of high T and low IQ is shaping up to be the most significant social challenge of the twenty-first century. Sturdy young men used to find jobs doing hard manual labour. What will they do when the muscle jobs have disappeared?

Plenty of people think there's way too much T in the world already and we'd be better off with less of it. So far, no one has suggested a way to bring that about (or at least, not a way that men would go for). But in case you want more of it for yourself, you can now get it in a tube. That's right: testosterone gel. Just rub it on and feel the surge. If you think Viagra's big, just wait.

Busy, Busy, Busy

Not long ago, I phoned up an old friend of mine, a high-powered career woman who is usually on the road two or three days a week.

"How about lunch?" I said. "How does your calendar look for June?"

"How about today?" she said. "I'm totally free."

I was shocked. Nobody I know is free for lunch today. A person of average busyness is sometimes free the week after next. If you're trying to book a higher-status person, four to six weeks is normal, by which time you will be lucky to remember what it is you wanted to have lunch about anyway. This lunch will probably be rearranged a few times by various executive assistants, who will spend more time talking to each other, coordinating your respective calendars, than you will spend talking to your lunchee. If you are higher status (i.e., busier) than the other person, you will be allowed to reschedule at least twice.

That is, if you still do lunch. Busy people don't, and when they do, they tell you, "I really don't do lunch anymore," implying that you ought to be immensely honoured that they have broken the rule for you. And you'd better eat in a hurry. An hour and ten minutes is the most anyone spends on a business lunch now.

Whenever I run into someone I haven't seen for a while and ask how they are, they always say the same thing: "I'm really busy."

Want to get together for dinner some Saturday with another busy couple? Two months, minimum, before you can fit it in.

And when you do get together, you'll all brag about how much e-mail you get. "It's horrible," someone will say. "I took three days off and when I got back to the office I had six hundred e-mails!"

"That's nothing," the next person will say. "I had two thousand, and I had forty-seven voice mails."

The truly busy person, of course, will have answered all these voice mails and e-mails while on vacation so that she can get right back down to work.

Then comes the discussion about how early people get up in the morning. If you sleep in after 5:30 on a weekday, your best strategy is to lie about it so your friends don't think you're a slacker.

Recently, I took a few days off from work between assignments. It was pleasant to spend all day reading the papers at my kitchen table, with the sun streaming in, no places to go, no people to see. Pleasant—for about five minutes. Then I started to get nervous. What if they had forgotten all about me? So I got on the phone and called a few friends. The first person I called had to take a call on his cellphone while he was speaking to me. The second and third persons were in meetings and would call me back just as soon as they were free.

Everyone was so busy! I recalled that just the day before I had been that busy too, and in a few days' time I would be that busy again. Meantime, I had the odd sensation that I was fading away. I quickly invented a ridiculously complicated project that involved a great deal of Internet searching and faxing things overseas at all hours of the day and night, and immediately felt much better.

How did we get so busy? That's not too hard to figure out. The work world has become a far more Darwinian place in the past decade. Plenty of middle managers with middling incomes are obligated to put in sixty or seventy hours a week on the job. Workaholism? It's a condition of employment. Job flexibility? Puh-lease. New technology? Fabulous. It lets us work all the time. To be is to do. And the more there is on your to-do list, the more reassured you are that you must count for something.

Of course, you don't get work overload without work stress, and everyone I know has plenty of that. But people who suddenly aren't busy have more.

One man told me what happened to him after he had accepted a gigantic buyout. He took his bag of money and set up a little office to figure out what to do next. He showed up on Monday morning at eight. His appointment book was blank. The phone didn't ring. Nobody needed him. He says it was the worst moment of his life.

When I met my friend for lunch, I asked her what had happened to her ultra-busy schedule. She told me that she had put herself on a strict new regimen. She was turning down at least three assignments a week. She was practising being a slacker. She had sworn off multitasking and was trying unitasking, though she confessed it was incredibly difficult. Then she invited me to go to the garden centre with her after lunch.

It would have been fun, I said. But I really had to get back to work.

Breaking the Cycle: An Addict's Tale

After half a working life in management, I realized I was in the wrong end of the media business. In journalism, it's the writers who have all the fun. No meetings. No budgets. No people to hire and fire. No new publishers to break in. After I made the switch to full-time writing, I wondered what on earth had taken me so long. But at first it was a shock. No one in the office bothered talking to me anymore, except to warn me that I'd better file on time, or else.

It seemed to me that there ought to be some self-help group I could join to aid in my transition to a more normal life. We would all get together to share our experiences, and I could make a speech like this: "Hello. My name is Margaret W., and I am a recovering workaholic. I'm proud to tell you that, today, I didn't get to the office until 11:48."

I spent more than twenty years in middle management. In all those years, I never went a day without a meeting. I quit cold turkey two years ago. But I still crave those meetings. Every day, I wonder what it would be like to have just one more.

When I was a kid, I could scarcely wait to work. I just wanted to grow up fast, I guess. I'll never forget my first business card. What a rush! When I got it, I called a meeting right away.

For many years, the only friends I had were heavy workers. We had a lot of fun together. Working made me feel less shy and more gregarious. It was the first thing I thought about when I woke up, and the last thing I thought about before I closed my eyes at night. I confess I often worked before breakfast.

My husband? Hah! He loved it even more than I did. Sometimes, he'd work all night until he blacked out. Once or twice I tried to erase his computer files, but he always found them and rebooted them. And, secretly, I egged him on. I figured that so long as he was working more than me, I wasn't working too much.

The average Canadian works 42.2 hours a week, or so they say. Personally, I think people lie about it—fifty, sixty, seventy hours was just a warm-up for me. In twenty years, I never missed a special project or a task force. Weekend management retreats. Unpaid Sunday overtime. Corporate strategy sessions, awards banquets, executive development school, client appreciation nights, farewell lunches, team-building exercises—you name it, I never missed a single one.

When I was in management, people competed to see who could work the most. One time I worked eighteen days in a row. But that was nothing. Once I saw a woman file a story as they were wheeling her into the delivery room to give birth. I'd like to see a man match that.

Still, I found that plenty of men could outwork me. If I sent my e-mails at 7:09 a.m., the sales manager would send his e-mails at 5:15. One day, I got to work to find an e-mail from the CEO of the entire North American operation. He sent it to me at 3:13 a.m. I think that's when I knew I'd hit the wall.

One day soon after that, I snuck out of the office at three o'clock to meet my friend Laurie at the movies. Laurie had been recently outplaced, and I was just doing it to cheer her up. But she wasn't sad at all. In fact, she seemed transformed. Her haunted, driven look was gone. When she told me she'd had time to get her toenails done, I was sick with envy. Of course, all I could think of was how soon I could get back to work. But after the movie, Laurie frogmarched me to a café and forced a glass of Chardonnay down my throat. "It's time for you to turn your life around. You must surrender to a Higher Power."

The next day, I went home at four-thirty. It was still light out. It was really scary.

It's tough to be a recovering workaholic in Toronto. The climate's mean, so half the year there's nothing else to do. The city's ancient strain of Scottish Protestantism renders much of the populace genetically vulnerable to overwork. Besides, the culture has a deeply anhedonic streak. That's why Torontonians are chronically on time and gobble tuna-on-rye in front of their computer screens.

In my circle, overachievement is endemic. Friends get up at five so they can meet their personal trainer by six so they can get to work by seven-thirty, et cetera. Their idea of relaxation is training for a marathon. Their idea of downtime is going to a health spa, where they can hike fifteen miles a day, eat raw vegetables and proofread the 600-page textbook they just wrote on condominium law.

These people don't take vacations. They attack them. They believe that vacations should be self-improvement projects, that they should come back a better person. They never just go to the lake and drink beer.

Perhaps it was on some highly overscheduled trip to France that I began to glimpse the way that life could be. Perhaps it was the sight of people laughing in cafés at three p.m., drinking wine in business suits. They even had their cellphones off. I was astonished to learn the French do not believe in working while eating.

Or perhaps it was in Spain, where people have lunch till three or four and then take a nap, then go out at nine and smoke and drink till dinner, which starts at ten-thirty or eleven. Or in Bali, where they all skip work on holy days (which occur quite frequently) to sing and dance and put flowers in their hair. Or in the Caribbean, where entire islands are overrun by jolly Germans burning off their six weeks of statutory holidays.

I owe a lot to Laurie, who has become my personal coach in strategic laziness. With her help, I'm taking all of next week off. There's just one more all-day corporate meeting I have to go to first. Just one more. That's it. I promise.

Chapter Five

Roughing It in the Bush, con Latte

Like lots of stressed-out urbanites, my husband and I dreamed about escaping from our busy, busy lives. One day, we promised each other, we would leave the deadlines and the traffic behind and seek out the peace and quiet of the country. There we would plant a vegetable garden, wake up to the birds and enjoy the simple pleasures of rural life.

It didn't quite turn out that way. But then again, what does?

Buying a piece of country land is a little like getting pregnant. It is a leap into the unknown, a roll of the dice, a decision best taken in ignorance, and an interesting test of the marital relationship.

It's also an excuse for all your friends to share their favourite horror stories. Like the one about the people who drilled down 270 feet and still couldn't find water. And when they did, it was brown and smelly. "Drilling your well will cost you a hundred dollars a foot," they say with glee.

Or, "Too bad about Bob and Connie. They went hundreds of thousands over budget. The architect and the builder nearly killed each other. Then Bob and Connie nearly killed each other. Then the builder went bankrupt."

Or, "That new hydro line is going to run you thirty thousand, I bet."

Fortunately, there are plenty of local people who are eager to share their knowledge and expertise with city folks. "Sure is windy up here," they say when they come round to size up this or that. "Yep. Howls in from the northwest, all winter long. You'll have drifts as high as the house. Heh, heh."

The urge for country land is something primal. It is also Nature's way of parting city dwellers from their surplus capital, which they might otherwise throw away on Nortel shares. Instead, they can throw it away on something tangible. Which, in our case, amounted to fifty-three acres of the worst farmland this side of Georgian Bay. Too many hills and rocks. When last it changed hands a generation ago, it fetched a few pennies an acre and the farmer was glad to unload it.

Now this stony soil is caught up in the greatest land rush since the suburbs were built. Country property markets are catching fire all across North America. Those irritating baby boomers are at it again, snatching up the very same land their great-grandpas and grandmas happily abandoned for a better life in town.

Born-again country folks like to play at the same chores by which their forebears eked out a mean and bare subsistence.

And they're willing to pay dearly for the privilege. We have a weekend cow breeder nearby who in real life is a successful lawyer. Up the road is a banker who grows garlic. Down the road is another banker who runs a tree farm.

There's a publisher who's a part-time cowboy. He herds cattle just for fun. He lives in a barn which was carefully dismantled many miles away and remantled in the middle of a picturesque forest. It's been in magazines. It didn't really cost all that much more than a regular house.

There are people who muck stables and people who ride tractors and people who clear brush and people who grow heritage potatoes and raise angora goats. You can tell these people from local people because they are extremely proud of all the things the local people complain about. "The weather really is awful up here," they brag. "In winter, you can get snowed in for days." But not to worry. They're always well stocked with rosemary focaccia and beans from Starbucks.

Being city people, we had no idea what size an acre was. In the city, we measure land in feet. Fifty-three acres seemed more than anyone could possibly need for anything, but in a way that was the point. We bought it, mostly sight unseen, in the depths of winter.

"What an adventure you'll have discovering it all!" our friends enthused. They were right. After the snow melted, we walked through our woods and discovered ten or twenty thousand newly dead trees. Over the winter a big wind had blown through and knocked them over. We discovered vast tracts of impenetrable bush bearing large, needle-like spikes that ripped our flesh. We discovered a swamp that materialized suddenly in the spring where we thought our driveway was going to be. We discovered it when we drove into it and the car sank.

These days, swamps are called "wetlands," and you drain them at your peril. If your land is in an environmentally protected zone, various conservation officials exercise tyrannical control over your every move. Chop down a tree and you're dead. Dig a pond without asking them and they'll throw you in jail. We hope they don't find out about the swamp.

One of the delights of the country is the wildlife. It's everywhere. For example, we have tent caterpillars as far as the eye can see. I even stepped on a porcupine corpse in the woods, quills still bristling. "What could kill a porcupine?" I asked my husband, but he was flummoxed too. One lifetime is not long enough to unlock Nature's secrets.

If the conservation officials will let us, our dream is to build a modest little shack with whatever remains of our credit line. So what if we have to row in from the road? There are bidding wars now for land like this. Everyone tells us our investment will go up. We look at it this way: if each square foot of our country land was worth what our city land is worth, we could sell it for $527 million. Not that we ever would. Our heart is in the country now. We could even get a cow.

The Simple Life Does Not Come Cheap

When we fell in love with country life, we discovered that a charming old authentic farmhouse does not come cheap. So we decided to build a new one from scratch. Building your own home is one of life's greatest thrills, and it's not as hard as it looks. First you dig a hole and throw in all your money. Then you borrow every cent you can. Then you go 100 per cent over budget. But it's worth it to get exactly what you want. Your canvas is uncompromised. No putting up with someone else's shoddy work or dreadful taste. No dreary bathroom tile just like the guy next door's. Every detail of your dream home can express your unique desires and sensibilities, providing you can figure out what they are.

Take toilets. Many people make the mistake of thinking that toilets are pretty much the same, but we know better. We've seen them all. We went to Home Depot and spent hours with the toilet man. We made several trips to Ginger's Bath Centre and compared the comfort of the seats. We even cruised the Web. We debated different styles and tank capacities. We were determined to find that precise nexus of aesthetics, environmental awareness, flushability and price point. After all, you only buy your toilets once. Finally, we settled on a brand called Toto. "Is it art or is it science?" teased the headline on the Toto toilet brochure. Surprise! It was both.

The toilets were just a warm-up. After them, we moved on to sinks and faucets. (Four- or eight-inch? Single or double? Chrome or satin or nickel? Gooseneck? Lever or cross handle? Plastic insides or brass?) Bravely, we pressed on, struggling to develop rational preferences for items and choices we had never known existed. Window research consumed us for many agonizing weeks. Next came flooring materials and finishes, cabinets and closets, counters and light fixtures, major appliances and grills and handles and switchplates and nineteen thousand different paint colours.

Mostly we managed to agree, but sometimes not. Our marriage nearly foundered on marmoleum. I forget exactly why, or what marmoleum is, but at the time it was the most important thing on earth.

And we grew strangely perverse. Sometimes, nothing was good enough for us. Since everybody else has ordinary doorknobs, we decided we must have thumblatches. We scoured the province. We phoned antique thumblatch dealers. No luck. After months of searching, we found some in a catalogue and had them shipped from Massachusetts. They cost ten times more than ordinary doorknobs, but we convinced ourselves that nothing else would do. This is why people go 100 per cent over budget.

One day the inevitable crack-up came. It was the day the man who built the kitchen cabinets dropped by. "You've got to choose your cabinet knobs!" he ordered cheerily, and gave me three or four thick catalogues filled with thousands of different possibilities. You could get porcelain knobs, or solid gold knobs, or little handles shaped like forks and knives. In a daze, I spent hours trying to decide. I sought advice from all my friends. But I had hit the wall. "Do whatever you want," I begged the kitchen-cabinet man, and so he did.

Choice is supposed to be enriching. Maybe so, but it also makes us slaves. "Often, we use choice to define who we are," says Frances Cairncross, the British writer who identified this uniquely modern affliction.

So there it is. Every time we flush, we know that we are Toto toilet people, and all our friends know it too. "Runs silent, runs deep," my husband brags. Secretly, we pity people who don't have one, and feel subtly superior.

Everything Old Is New Again

Once our new country house was finished, we wanted to get it to look old, as if Susanna Moodie might once have lived there. We wanted a rustic, authentic kind of pioneering look. My husband called it "instant roots."

"Plain, honest, old wood furniture," we agreed. "That's what we need. Built with their hands by real people." Factory-made furniture would not do. We wanted a big homemade harvest table that looked as if the dog had chewed on it.

You can't get this type of furniture from farmers anymore. They've got rid of all their old junk and bought nice stuff from Sears. And so our first stop was a dusty antique barn in the country. "Harvest tables," snorted the proprietor. "Very hard to find these days." He showed us one that cost $7,800, but it was sold already.

Our new house had no closets (we wanted the rustic look), so we also needed some old armoires to put our clothes in. One day we stopped at a place that was highly recommended by my friend Barbara, who has a harvest table I would kill for. Right away I spied a big beat-up old armoire with crooked feet and old paint flecks and a wooden peg to hold the doors shut. It listed sharply to one side. "Perfect!" I exclaimed. I looked for the price tag, and it said $22,000.

I have discovered that old paint flecks are extremely valuable.

Fortunately, if you can't afford them, you can make your own. You apply some milk paint (sixteen dollars a litre), then cover it with a substance called crackle, then cover that with more milk paint. Presto! You now have a piece of furniture that looks like the kind poor people threw in the dump as soon as they could afford to trade up.

City people like the aged and weathered look because it gives authenticity to things. You can pretend they (and you) have a history. To get your new house to look old, you should use dark glaze to paint the corners of your rooms and the walls along your door jams—anywhere dirt and grime would naturally collect. You can also buy a stain the colour of nicotine.

I know these things because I'm addicted to shelter magazines—what my husband calls "decor porn." They're crammed with tips on how to acquire the distressed look. Use a wire brush to rough up your kitchen hardware. Have your counter made of zinc or marble, then pour red wine on it and scratch it with a knife. Do your floor in mismatched pine boards with lots of saw marks. Bash it up a bit and stain it to look old. You want it to look as if you salvaged the wood from Susanna Moodie's house.

It's all a cheat, of course. Authentic authenticity is beyond most people's means. I dream of floors made of two-hundred-year-old virgin heart pine recovered from airless bogs by scuba divers and re-milled to leave the ancient nail holes and worm tracks intact. But only stockbrokers can have that. I'll have to settle for faking it.

The current fashion trend is for the very rich to emulate the very poor, despite the cost. In the countryside north of Toronto, the very rich live in rebuilt old barns. In Santa Fe, they live in houses made of mud. There are three kinds of adobe houses in the Southwest: there are the simple ones made of dried mud, where a few impoverished indigenous people still dwell; there are the tasteful stucco houses of the middle class, which only look like dried mud; and there are the real adobe mansions of the very rich, which must be re-mudded every year. A real mud mansion is the ultimate status symbol.

David Brooks, author of the seminal book *Bobos in Paradise*, calls this trend for the rich to adopt the markers of the poor "status inversion." Your consumption patterns must be conspicuously inconspicuous. A preference for the plain and simple is a sign of your refreshing, unaffected honesty and distances you from ostentatious yuppies.

In home decor, natural materials are essential to project unaffected honesty. You must have sisal rugs, even though they hurt your feet. Flowers on the table are too contrived these days. Tasteful people have a wedge of grass.

If you want an outdoor fence or screen, you should make it out of dry stone stacked by Mennonites. If you don't have Mennonites, you could try a fence of willow, which you can learn to harvest and weave yourself. If you're too pressed for time, you can hire the Willow Lady, who lives near us and will weave it for you. But I warn you that she's very busy these days. She recently wove an eighty-foot-long willow wall for someone's country house. It cost two hundred dollars a foot.

Not surprisingly, our farming neighbours think we're odd. We build our houses on the hills, where the winter wind howls down on us. They build their houses near the roads, so they don't have to plow a kilometre of laneway. Most of them gave

up their drafty old farmhouses long ago for sensible bunga-
lows made of brick. They have broadloom on their floors, not
pine planks. They are amazed at how much we'll pay for a cup
of coffee and for battered-up old junk.

We haven't found the harvest table of our dreams yet. But we
did get a beat-up old desk that we made into a washstand. It
seems to have been used for stacking paint cans. When we
bought it, there was some manure and straw stuck to its legs,
so it was definitely in a real barn. It cost us only slightly more
than a fancy bathroom sink from Ginger's. And it's much
more honest.

The Ghost of Susanna Moodie

Of course, we only play at wanting to live like Susanna
Moodie. We wouldn't survive her life for five minutes. An
intrepid Englishwoman who was also attracted by the romantic myth of rustic living, she left her genteel world to strike out
for Canada in 1834. It took her months to get here. The last leg
of her journey was by horse-drawn sleigh through the deep
woods. The sleigh overturned in the frozen night, and her
cherished Coalport tea service was smashed to bits. Those
teacups were her last link to civilization.

Today our rustic country retreats are kitted out with every
modern convenience. A neighbour of ours has installed seven
wide-screen TVs in his luxury barn. Our idea of roughing it is
doing without a satellite dish. "We only get four channels," we
brag. But there is a video rental store at every country cross-

roads. On frozen winter nights, we stoke the wood fire high, just for the fun of it, and watch a rented DVD.

Sometimes I think of Susanna and her sister Catharine Parr Traill giving birth to babies in the bush, struggling to grow enough food to feed their families and scribbling their romantic tales late into the night by the light of smoky tallow candles. They didn't write because they had a craving to express themselves. They wrote because they needed the money. They were immensely tougher than we will ever be. They both survived their feckless husbands and lived until a ripe old age, long enough to see the frontier recede and much of the bush be cut down. What would they make of their modern sisters and our soft and comfy lives? Would they envy us? I don't think so. I think they would say we fatally lack character.

The Flowers That Bloom in the Spring, Ha Ha

When spring finally came to our country retreat (weeks after bulbs had already bloomed in the city), our thoughts turned to the great outdoors. "I want a beautiful meadow all around us," I told my husband. The hottest trend in country gardening is a natural wildflower meadow ablaze with charming native specimens. Everybody has to have one. Ours would be just like a real meadow, only better. It would be a sort of essence of meadow, with all the bad things deleted and all the good things enhanced. It would be entirely natural, only with better taste.

And so we set to work. We ordered six cubic yards of topsoil (because our real dirt wasn't good enough). We shovelled it and levelled it, rototilled it and rolled it. And then we planted. Don't ask me what the month of June was like that year, because I spent it on my knees. We dreamed of drifts of meadow flowers bobbing in the breeze.

Then came July. A mysterious form of crabgrass began to sprout. Every clump grew three feet high and three feet wide. Apparently it had come with the topsoil. Don't ask me what August was like, because I spent August pulling it out. "Wait till next year," my husband promised.

The next year we had drifts. We had drifts of dandelions, and then of giant thistles with stalks as thick as wrists, and of a mysterious weed that's too strong to pull up by the roots. The hundreds of innocent little plants we had so tenderly placed in among the thugs were not to be found. They got mugged.

The lesson we learned is that Nature is not naturally benign. Only city people need to learn this. Country people have spent their entire lives wrestling Nature to the ground. They know that if you want to live in harmony with Nature, you've got to show it who's boss. It must be whipped and hacked and burned into submission. Strong chemicals are an asset.

"How can you possibly improve on Nature?" my friends sigh as they gaze out over the hills and fields and streams that decorate their weekend places. But the truth is, they can't help improving on it. They want a better Nature than Nature will provide. The high standards they set for their aesthetic experience of the countryside ensure that their weekends are an endless round of drudgery and toil. One of my friends spent his entire summer vacation dragging dead branches out of his woods. He says they make the woods look messy. He wants his woods tidied up and clutter-free. Now I'm ashamed to show him around our woods because they're so unkempt. They are full of rot and dead things. On its own, Nature is not nearly neat enough.

The trouble with achieving the natural effect is that it's not relaxing. It takes steady effort, discipline and vigilance, and gobs of money don't hurt either.

Some friends of ours have hired a team of trained wild-flower professionals, who claim they can naturalize a small meadow for around $10,000. We're saving up our money so that someday we can naturalize our meadow too.

Have I Got a Tomato for You

Unlike charming native wildflowers, the great thing about tomatoes is that any idiot can grow them. What could be finer than biting into that first ripe, red tomato that you have grown and watered all by yourself? The thing about tomatoes that takes craft and guile is disposing of them.

"Maybe I'll take a pass," my husband whinged one week in September after I had served him tomatoes for thirty-eight days in a row. I told him to shut up and eat. It would be a crime to let them go to waste.

I gave away hundreds of tomatoes to my friends, but the tomatoes just kept on coming. After I ran out of friends, I decided to make tomato sauce. I found a fancy tomato press at Williams-Sonoma and took it home. By the time I was done, my kitchen looked like the set of *The Texas Chainsaw Massacre*.

But I accomplished my objective—I had enough tomato sauce to last six years.

My friend Suzanne always has several bushels of garden vegetables she's hoping to unload. Her biggest cucumber was a metre long and had a peculiar curve in it. I suggested that maybe she could keep it and start a fertility cult. Or she could use it to club her enemies to death (it's as heavy as a baseball bat), then shred the evidence and serve it up for dinner. She could commit the perfect crime.

What is the impulse that compels us to grow food we don't need then invent ways to use it up? It's not frugality. Buying tomatoes at the supermarket would be cheaper than the dirt I had to buy to grow my own in. My mother, a notorious vegetable-grower, blames the Depression. I blame our hunter-gatherer brains, which are hardwired to believe that we will starve if we don't put food up for the winter.

Perhaps this is why I can't bear to throw out even one tomato. I'd rather let it sit in the bottom of the vegetable bin until it rots into a puddle of mouldy goo.

There's another reason to grow things you don't need. It reminds you that you are actually capable of producing something you can smell and touch. Not many of us have that experience anymore. We toil away in our symbol-manipulation factories, creating bits and bytes that we exchange for other bits and bytes that we exchange for food at Loblaws.

We have become grotesquely overspecialized creatures, capable of writing newspaper columns or trading in exotic bonds but helpless as infants in supplying the necessities of our own life.

I can neither sew nor spin, build a house nor bale some hay.

The only useful thing I can do is poke a hole in a pile of dirt and put a tomato plant in it.

People are so guilty about throwing out produce that they will go to ridiculous lengths to use it up. The other day, somebody gave a giant zucchini to my friend Cindy. She should have snuck it into the compost heap when that person wasn't looking. But no, she put it in the blender and made forty cups of shredded squash. Then she went to the store and got three dozen eggs and thirty dollars worth of chocolate chips, and spent the next eleven hours baking. Now she has two dozen loaves of zucchini bread that she's desperate to unload. I told her I'd swap her some tomato sauce for it.

Tomato sauce isn't the only substance we have a surplus of. One fall my husband was overcome by an urge to make hard cider. So he went out and bought six bushels of apples and found an antique cider press retrofitted with a two-stroke diesel engine.

He set up the cider press outside on a blustery fall day. What you do is put the apples in the top, mash them up in the middle and catch the juice as it runs out of the bottom. This is fun if you like being splattered from head to toe with frozen apple mush. After that, he put the juice in a vat and fooled around with it in the basement for a few months until it started to ferment. Then he poured it into special beer bottles that he had spent weeks scrounging from liquor stores.

Today, we have a basement full of cider (minus the bottles that, unhappily, exploded). My husband is extremely proud of it, and we always offer it to all our friends. To be truthful, it's a bit of an acquired taste. But it's a great way to use up extra apples.

Just about everybody we know has some special project that's gotten out of hand. My friend Jane has an entire room crammed with bottles of beans and beets and pickles from her garden. We have another friend named Norm who recently bought sixty chickens. He says he got a good deal on them. Now Norm has more eggs than he can possibly get rid of, so he carries them around in the back of his car to give away to anyone he meets. This makes him happy.

And now we've got honey. A neighbour down the road has a bunch of bees, and my husband asked if he could help out with them. He bought himself a bee suit, and before long he came home with thirty pounds of honey fresh from the hive. I have no idea how we're going to use it up, but he doesn't seem too concerned. He's going to unload some on his poker buddies. And then he's going to learn how to make mead.

What's Not to Love about My SUV?

Call me criminal. But my neighbours don't. They remember how we plucked them from the elements one stormy winter night on a remote country road. Their puny little car couldn't make it up the hill. We overtook them in our SUV as they were flailing through the drifts on foot. They were wearing their city shoes. We gave them a lift home. They never asked us "What would Jesus drive?" Now they've got an SUV, too.

It's high time for SUV owners to unite and strike back. We've helped dig you out, and we've taken enough of your abuse.

Contrary to what you may have read, SUV drivers are the

opposite of vain, self-absorbed and arrogant. On the contrary. We're plugged into Canada's deepest values. Read your Margaret Atwood: this country is all about survival. We've got more wilderness than any other nation in the world. We've got wilderness embedded in our souls. We've also got a lot of really nasty weather. In my view, the SUV ought to be declared Canada's official vehicle.

And don't tell me about high gas prices. (It's funny that the people who want to ban gas-guzzlers are the same people who demand price caps whenever gas goes over eighty cents.) Buying lots of gas is patriotic. All those nice oil revenues have helped make our country rich, and we won't run out of the stuff for another thousand years or so.

I guess I could live with being called vain, self-absorbed and arrogant. But I draw the line at being called a natural-born killer. Writing in the *Globe,* an SUV-hater named Laura Robinson related how appalled she was to witness two incidents in which SUVs "nearly hit" women pushing baby strollers. According to her, this is why there's no world peace. "The nasty people who consider it unnecessary to watch for human beings on the sidewalk aren't that far removed from the ones now plotting war," she concluded.

People who dump on SUVs are like mullahs who have appointed themselves the guardians of public morality. They're public scolds who think that conspicuous consumption is vulgar and having fun is worse. They're the type of people who snoop into your garbage to see if you recycle. If they catch you taking the kids to McDonald's, they think it's child abuse.

Deep down inside, these people really believe all cars are

wicked. They think all of us should get around on bikes and public transit. In their view, people who love cars for the freedom and mobility they bring (to say nothing of the six-CD players and heated leather seats) are like people in the olden days who had sex for fun—dangerous and immoral.

By the way, what *would* Jesus drive? It's not hard to figure out. Jesus was a country carpenter. So if he lived in Canada, he'd drive an old, beat-up F-150 pickup, which is the vehicle of choice up in our neck of the woods. If he was a really successful carpenter, he'd drive a 250. And some of his disciples would turn them into mudders with gigantic tires and extra strong suspensions, and in winter they'd dig out the Pharisees from the big city for fifty bucks a pop.

As it happens, pickup trucks get the worst emissions ratings of anything on the road. And they outsell SUVs by a country mile. But if Ms. Robinson ever dares to wag her righteous finger at the country carpenters, they'll just tell her to hose off.

A Taste of Morel Victory

Anyone who moves to the country from the city is in for culture shock: they do things differently there. For instance, country people think we are insane to pay $3.95 for a cup of caffeinated foamy milk. They eat dinner promptly at six, and feel genuinely sorry for anyone who has to live in Toronto and breathe in all that smog.

But country life is not laid back. *Au contraire.* It, too, has status markers and ruthless competitions. Instead of Beemer envy, people have tractor envy. Even weekenders have to have tractors. There's nothing like a shiny $9,000 John Deere with lots of attachments to make you feel as if you're living the authentic life.

And May marks the most ruthless competition of them all. May is Morel Month in Ontario. And everybody in the country knows that morels are serious business. Friendships are one thing; morels are another.

For example, I've known my neighbour, Hugh, for years. I know almost all his secrets. But I don't know where his morels are. All I know is that he shows up each May with heaps of shiny black ones, gloating. All his friends have tried to find out where he gets them, but he's not telling.

In case you're mycologically challenged, morels are fungi. They pop up in the woods in spring. They have an elongated cap that's wrinkled like a brain, and a pleasant nutty flavour. My husband and I spent years hunting for morels without finding any. "What's your secret?" I begged Hugh, who is a Buddhist.

"The secret is that if you're looking for them, you won't find them," he said. As you can see, morel-hunting is very Zen-like.

Morel-hunting is also a major escalation of the food-status stakes. Organic is all very well, but everybody does organic nowadays. Today, the highest-status food is food that you've foraged for yourself. Forget farming—we're talking hunting and gathering.

Near us in the country is a very popular restaurant with a celebrity chef. It's famous far and wide for its natural, organic and wild food. Even Greenpeace has endorsed it. People book months ahead and drive two hours each way from the city in their SUVs to enjoy its earth-friendly approach to dining, which costs only $150 a person (plus gas and wine). They eat trout from spring-fed ponds, tender dandelion greens, edible flowers, venison, fiddleheads and fungi, and they discover what sturdy self-reliance and living off the land are really all about. Sometimes the chef even leads people through the woods so they can forage for themselves.

Our friends Bob and Melissa (who live the simple country life in a designer barn) have a field of wild asparagus. We're sick with envy because we don't have one. Every spring, they invite us to help ourselves to the tiny little stalks that poke up through the ground. (Like morels, the wild asparagus is unavoidably phallic.) We compete to see who can snap off the most tender shoots. I always lose, because they're hard to see in the grass. "Stop looking," says Hugh, "and you'll see more."

There's something undeniably primal about foraging for food. It makes you feel ruggedly self-sufficient. It also gets you outside, which is more than you can say for Loblaws. Best of all is the thrill of the hunt. You never know when you're going to hit the motherlode. Every year, as we chow down on our morel omelettes, morel risottos and steak morel, we feel incredibly superior. After all, other people are actually paying forty or fifty dollars a pound for these things.

My own morel triumph occurred last year. It was after I had given up. I had looked for days, but obviously I wasn't sufficiently spiritually evolved. And then I saw it—a giant patch, in plain view right by the road. I shrieked and fell on them. I was with some city people who'd never heard of morels and thought I was demented. I stuffed my pockets full, swore my companions to secrecy and took my haul to show it off to Hugh.

I made a giant morel risotto for all my friends, and I could tell they were impressed. We sat around and fantasized about living off the land if the Depression ever comes back. We would gather mushrooms from the woods and watercress from the ponds, berries from the meadows and wild apples from the roadside. We would keep bees and chickens. We'd go wild-turkey shooting in the summer and deer hunting in the fall, just like the country people do. (Not Hugh, though. He's a vegetarian.)

But it's hard to keep up with the Buddhists. The last time I saw Hugh, he was bragging about his ramps. I had to ask him what they were. Ramps, he told me, are a kind of wild leek that you find in the woods in spring, and they're the latest thing in foraging. Of course, you have to know where to look. Or else you can pay $150 to eat them at the famous restaurant up the road.

As I said, the country people think we're insane.

Getting Back to Nature Bites

Down the road from our place in the country, the neighbours have thrown in the towel. I'll be sorry to see them go. They bought the house a couple of years ago because they liked the clean air and the splendid views. Nobody told them about the wind, which howls down from the northwest and peels the paint right off a place.

Then came winter. The snow started falling in November and lingered until May. "Snowiest winter we ever had around here," the farmers said. The second winter, their hill turned into a sheet of ice. They were trapped for days. Now they've put up a For Sale sign. They dreamed of going back to Nature, and Nature got the best of them.

In the magazines devoted to the charms of country living (and I've read them all), Nature has been heavily made over and retouched. The real Nature is not a pretty thing. As one old farmer says whenever a nasty storm blows up, "She's a hooer."

City folks have no idea, of course. When we acquired our little patch of country land, I was in love. I overlooked the swamp and thornbush. Once spring came, I would gambol barefoot through the flower-sprinkled meadow, gathering nosegays. I would wear a gauzy linen dress and a jaunty straw hat. After gambolling, my love and I would picnic by the pond in a bee-loud glade. In the distance, sheep would safely graze.

Now I know better.

Anyone who gambols in my meadow in the month of May is first advised to don a bug suit. This item is not featured in the glossy pages of *Country Living* or the bucolic rhapsodies of Wordsworth and Thoreau. Nonetheless, it is essential. Without it, the blackflies will tear out chunks of your flesh. You will bleed profusely on your linen, and you will swell up like a turnip.

In the country, we know that summer has arrived when the blackflies make way for the mosquitoes. (West Nile virus, anyone?) You can ditch the bug suit, but you should not venture into Nature unless you're swathed in several coats of DEET. I soon discovered that no matter how I longed to embrace Nature, she had no desire to embrace me back. In fact, Nature acts as if she'd like me to bugger off.

The view of the natural world as a sort of benign, ennobling spirit from whose bosom mankind has been untimely wrenched is held only by people who don't actually have to live there. For the rest of us, it's mortal combat—a relentless race with Nature to undo whatever havoc she has wrought while you weren't looking. This race is not for wimps or nice guys. In the country, we don't do organic. We do Killex.

Our other projects have left us similarly pressed for gambolling time. Somebody must remove the trees the wind blew down into the bee-loud glade. Somebody must figure out why the brand-new pond we had dug at vast expense is leaking. Somebody must gas up the chainsaw, then hunt for all the bits and pieces of it when a nut falls off and the chainsaw flies apart. Somebody must dig out the person underneath the tree that fell the wrong way when he tried to cut it down and the chainsaw got stuck in it.

In fairness, the somebody who gets saddled with this hard labour is usually my husband. As I frequently explain to him, I wasn't born to tame the wilderness. I was born to read the weekend papers.

As those who've gone before us have discovered, a foray into country life is invariably a test of a relationship. Some born-again country-lovers find out they're married to people who get a nosebleed if they venture north of the city limits. These differences are sometimes irreconcilable, to the great good fortune of country real-estate agents.

Despite our differences, my husband and I have been united by our common enemy. And we have worked out an understanding about how to divide the labour. I will deal with rodents if they're dead, but live ones are his job. Snakes and wasps' nests are his responsibility. Anything that requires dressing up in helmets, gauntlets, steel boots, bee suits and other funny costumes is up to him. Anything that involves jumping into the pond naked on a hot summer day is up to me. When at last we have our picnic, some weekend in September when the bugs are gone, the chores are done, the leak is fixed and all the thistles have been blasted to oblivion, I will make the lunch. We will inhale the fresh clean scent of Nature, unless the wind is blowing from the direction of the cattle operation. I will wear a gauzy linen dress and a straw hat, if it doesn't rain or snow or hail.

But you never know. She can be a hooer.

Chapter Six

The Mommy Track

One evening I got together with a couple of girlfriends for a glass of wine or three. All of us forgot to have kids. So I decided to conduct a focus group.

"Are you miserable?" I asked. "Does your grief come in layers of bitterness and regret because you missed out on Mother Nature's gift?"

They looked at me blankly.

"Maybe you need more Chardonnay to get in touch with your feelings," I suggested. But it was no good. Instead of getting in touch with their inner grief, they just kept on yakking about the Middle East and the South Beach diet. Finally, I had to confront them outright.

"According to the experts," I said, "there is an epidemic of misery among successful women because they never got around to having babies. It's the hidden social tragedy of our time. So confess already."

The person who diagnosed this epidemic is an economist named Sylvia Ann Hewlett, who wrote a best-selling book called *Creating a Life: Professional Women and the Quest for Children.* It spawned a whole genre of journalism devoted to this theme. Maybe you saw the cover story in *Time.* The cover featured a sad-looking woman with a baby blanket and a Palm Pilot where the baby was supposed to be. Or maybe you saw the item on *Sixty Minutes,* which featured a bunch of women with Harvard M.B.A.'s who couldn't even get a date. "Child-lessness," mourned Ms. Hewlett, "haunts the executive suite."

It's odd that no matter what choices women make, some-one's going to tell us we'll be very, very miserable. Single or married, childless or mothers, working for pay or working at home, someone's always going to say we got the short end of the stick. Back when I was single, the *Toronto Star* actually ran a story with the headline, "Singles Lead Lives of Quiet Despair That Sometimes Lead to Morgue."

But one thing is true about the trend Ms. Hewlett identified: we sure aren't having babies like we used to. And this fact is driving social planners crazy.

My family is entirely typical. My brother and sister have two kids each, but I don't have any. Neither does my youngest sis-ter. My other sister has four, and everybody thinks she's nuts. But I'm grateful to her. Without her heroic efforts, our family tree would completely shrivel up.

But most other families I know are shrinking too. Twenty per cent of women in my generation never bothered to have kids, and our nieces look like slackers too. The baby boom has given way to a boom in childlessness. And we all know what that means. Canada will soon be overrun by cranky senior citizens demanding pension cheques and hip replacements. Already, Depends are outselling Pampers. One top economist warned recently that an aging population is a "global hazard" on par with the atom bomb.

If you don't have children either, I hope you're feeling guilty now.

The experts, who are invariably men, used to believe that women's fertility rate would never fall below replacement levels (which means that every woman's quota is 2.1 kids). They were wrong. It turns out that women's innate need to nurture is rather easy to override. Women have decided that motherhood looks like a fairly crummy deal, compared with all the other deals on offer these days.

Naturally, we didn't plan it this way. Most of us did plan on kids, eventually, and most younger women still do. When you ask young adults how many children they want, almost all of them say two. But the national fertility rate has plunged to an all-time low of 1.5, which means that without help we'll all die out.

All around the world, men are trying to induce women to reproduce. Some nations are bribing them with bigger baby bonuses, free daycare and generous parental leaves. In Spain, government officials are going on the radio to appeal to women's patriotic sense of duty. In Japan, they are being told to be less selfish, like Princess Masako. In Sweden, tennis star Bjorn Borg took out a newspaper ad urging folks to procreate. The treasurer of Australia has promised $3,000 per infant in baby bonuses. "You go home and do your patriotic duty tonight," he told the nation. "You should have one for your husband, one for your wife and one for your country." In Canada, someone urged the government to launch a massive public relations campaign. After all, it worked for smoking.

Some people blame poverty for the birth dearth. They argue that families can't afford to have more children. Actually, affluence is to blame. Educated, urban women have fewer children than anybody else. The reason is something called "opportunity cost," which means the better off you are, the more you have to give up for motherhood.

In fact, if you treated motherhood as a rational decision, you'd never do it. At the very least, your social life will go to hell, and if you stay home to raise your kids you will be subjected to ruthless social demotion. One friend of mine told me that whenever she told a stranger at a party she was a stay-at-home mom, she was invariably dropped like a hot potato.

Social critics are wringing their hands over this epidemic of infertility. Critics from the right blame selfish modern secular society and the collapse of family values. "Many feminist women are unwittingly cheating themselves out of childbearing," grumped a man in a letter to the editor. "Women aren't being responsible toward the civilization to which they belong." They even worry that we are weakening the gene pool by refusing to reproduce. This fear goes back at least as far as Teddy Roosevelt, father of six, who warned, "If Americans of the old stock lead lives of celibate selfishness . . . disaster awaits the nation."

On the other side, social liberals blame faulty social policies and selfish men. If only we had universal daycare and better maternity leave, and if only men were more responsible for raising kids, all would be well.

So far, though, so-called family-friendly social policies have had zero impact on the birth rate. It turns out that the state is brilliantly successful at getting people to have fewer children, but no state has figured out how to persuade people to have more.

Most women these days put off motherhood until they finish their education, find the right partner and have a bit of economic security. Besides, they're not idiots. They know that the whole idea of work–life balance is a crock.

And so maybe the right time doesn't come until you're thirty-six. And by then, it's the wrong time, only you don't know it because nobody told you that your eggs are past their sell-by date. And most of the anxious couples clogging the fertility clinics go home empty-handed, although nobody told them the truth about that either. The legions of the childless (please don't say child-free, which makes children sound like a disease you catch) must console themselves with orderly houses, interesting work, trips to France, fine Chardonnay with their girlfriends and the stimulating company of other grown-ups.

Just ask my three-woman focus group. We all agreed that in spite of what the experts say, being childless has its compensations. All three of us wanted to have babies once, and we were disappointed when it didn't happen. But we recovered with unseemly haste. Our husbands, truth to tell, don't seem that disappointed in us either.

Maybe we're just shallow. Or maybe we know that anyone, man or woman, who claims to have it all in life is lying.

What's a Mother to Do?

Most kids' moms don't stay home anymore. The march of moms into the workforce is one of the biggest changes to the family in human history. Just twenty years ago, two-thirds of mothers with kids under three stayed home. Today, nearly two-thirds go to work. Among mothers of school-age kids, more than three-quarters go to work—the same percentage as women with no kids at all.

Why?

The common explanation is that they have to. Families need two incomes in order to make ends meet. Families say that if only they didn't need the money, Mom would work shorter hours and spend more time at home with the kids.

Don't believe it.

The mothers' guilty secret is that they love to work. And the money is the least of it. Work offers a whole host of rewards—intellectual, emotional and communal—that cannot be found at home in the company of your average three-year-old, no matter how delightful.

Not long ago, I spent an evening with 1,400 professional women who had gathered for an event called the Women of

Distinction Awards. This event is so popular that it's now held in the biggest meeting hall in Toronto. The room was crammed with mothers who are also lawyers, accountants, journalists, bankers, educators, communications consultants and human resources professionals. Most of them are terribly time-stressed and suffer pangs of guilt about not spending enough time with their kids. And not one in a hundred would willingly swap her job for a full-time stint at home.

Okay, so they're the elites. But it turns out that mothers in lower-level jobs feel the same. Sociology professor Arlie Russell Hochschild spent three years tracking ordinary working families with average jobs. What she found were workdays that stretch longer and longer, and women who work more and more overtime—by choice. She found that women hardly ever take advantage of family-friendly policies such as flextime, job sharing or the chance to work from home, and that the better off they are, the more true this is. The usual explanation is that people don't dare ask for time off or work-at-home days because they're afraid they'll somehow be penalized. The real reason, Ms. Hochschild concluded, is that on the whole they prefer to be at work.

She argues that for most of us, our primary social unit is no longer the family or the village but the workplace. Work is where we meet our friends, swap gossip, acquire our sense of identity and belonging. Chances are very high that our best friends at work know far more about our deepest joys and sorrows than our neighbours, or even most members of our immediate family.

In spite of layoffs and reorganizations, work provides more continuity and stability than current family life. These days, your relationship with your employer may well last longer than your relationship with your spouse. At the same time, Ms. Hochschild writes, "the emotional demands of family life have become much more baffling and complex." People aren't sure anymore what it takes to be a good mother, a good father, a good wife or husband. At work, the expectations are clear, and recognition and reward, thanks to enlightened managements, are increasingly common. The office has become a more enjoyable, less stressful place to be than home.

Meantime, there's less and less need for mothers to stay home, because there's less and less essential work to do there. Most of the drudge work that kept our great-grandmas in backbreaking servitude for sixteen hours a day has been automated and technologized nearly out of existence. No one has to spin wool, sew clothes, wash diapers, make soap, pump water, beat carpets, can vegetables, pluck chickens or bake bread, except as a hobby. Instant food is available everywhere. (Women's advocates complain that society devalues traditional women's work, but in truth there's not a lot to be said for it.)

What's left for a mother to do? Once upon a time mothers were also supposed to supervise the education and moral development of their small children and to run their social lives. Now there are professionals and experts to do that. Good mothers send their kids off to Montessori, Kumon and Suzuki so that they won't fall behind in the cognitive race. If a kid has emotional or behavioural problems, there are therapists and social workers.

All of this is not to argue for one moment that mothers love their children any less than they used to. Love (and guilt) are hard-wired into mothers. Just don't expect them to stay home with the kids, even if they can afford to.

I Was a Daycare Survivor

I am a product of unregulated daycare. When I was three, my mother enrolled me in Mrs. Reesor's Nursery School so that she could go out and type for a living. Mrs. Reesor was woefully unqualified. She had only one year of Normal School. The child-to-provider ratio was grotesque, since she also looked after five or six other kids. The outdoor play area (yard, dirt, grass, chain-link fence) was a severe safety hazard. As for stimulating our cognitive development, there was only Mrs. Reesor herself, thumping away on an old upright piano and leading us in lusty renditions of "America the Beautiful."

Today, Mrs. Reesor's nursery school would be shut down in a second, and my mother would be investigated for child neglect.

No subject is guaranteed to guilt out mothers like the daycare debate. Just take a look at those alarming headlines—"Most Places Are Mediocre or Worse, Study Finds," "Canadian Child Care Found 'Inadequate.'" And so on. It's enough to make any decent mom quit her job on the spot.

You might think these studies were funded by people who want to drive women back to the home. But no. The one that produced those scare quotes was funded by the federal government. Too bad, because it told thousands of parents and thousands of hard-working and underpaid caregivers that they're shortchanging their kids.

In fact, the real news is absolutely splendid. The study found that the vast majority of caregivers are warm, empathetic and nurturing and that the vast majority of care centres are safe and pleasant. The press release should have said, "Canada's Licensed Daycare Is the Very Best in the World."

So why didn't it? Because nobody would have paid any attention. And the authors of the report, well-meaning folks all, would not have had a hook to demand several billion dollars in more public money or a vast expansion of formal qualifications for professional caregivers. They seem to believe that your three-year-old is in grave danger unless the person looking after her has completed a four-year post-secondary program in early childhood education.

It makes you wonder how we managed to grow up at all.

Those dark conclusions are based on fashionable notions about brain development. According to the experts, your child's brain is a highly vulnerable organ, and if it isn't stimulated appropriately at crucial developmental stages, your kid will grow up to be an idiot.

"Given all the research on the potential of child care to encourage development and help prepare children for school, our findings represent a major lost opportunity," they say. "Zero to five are the most critical years in terms of child development."

Well, that's true. And so are the years six to ten, and eleven to seventeen. If it takes a village of caregivers with four years' post-secondary education to raise a child, we're in trouble.

The truth is that most kids manage to group up quite well without experts. An adequate environment with normal stimulation by kind and caring adults is all they need to get ready for school. It's true that kids from daycare often start out at school ahead of others, but the others catch up fast.

Children are remarkably resilient. It's harder to stunt them than to stimulate them. One brain expert says you practically have to lock them in a closet, cut off their food and hit them with a frying pan for years on end. It should be some comfort to know that your kids are likely to grow up fine despite you.

We do need to treat some kids better, especially poor ones. But the answer isn't to require caregivers to have advanced degrees and pile more regulations and restrictions and conditions on daycare centres, while warning parents of the perils of "unregulated, unlicensed" care. That will just push daycare costs out of sight, make parents anxious and make daycare even harder to find than it is now.

We should bring back Mrs. Reesor. We should stop guilting parents out.

The Hardest Choice of All

Every few years the abortion debate rolls round again. It never changes. As I drove across the city one steamy afternoon, the radio talk-show host was bawling out a woman caller. "Don't men ever get a say in this?" he yelled. "Are you telling me every woman should be free to abort her baby whenever she wants?"

Every so often, some crazy person plunges a knife into an

abortion doctor's back or takes a shot at him. Some doctors have stopped doing abortions because they're tired of the threats and the harassment. Some pharmacists say they won't sell the morning-after pill on moral grounds, and others say they won't sell it because, as one puts it, "we're not in a very good position to protect ourselves." Down south, most politicians have solemnly declared that they, personally, believe abortion is very wrong. Up here, some politicians say we shouldn't pay for it.

The guy on the radio was still ranting as I reached the Morgentaler clinic. I wanted to find out what life is like on the front lines.

The waiting room was behind two locked doors. It was busy. An Asian girl and a white boy were holding hands. There were several other young couples and a lot of singles. In another room, three clinic workers were on the phone booking appointments and soothing callers in various states of distress. Nearly all the patients were young enough to be my daughter. They looked like babies.

Jan, Barb and Sally have worked here for a long, long time. Jan and Barb are counsellors and Sally is a nurse.

"Who comes here? Everybody," says Barb.

"We're dealing with the entire world here," says Jan. "We see lawyers, and women in chains from jail. A lot of them are very surprised to be here."

"They never thought it would happen to them," says Sally.

They've seen it all. The eighteen-year-old who's already a single mom and pregnant again. The forty-eight-year-old who thought it was menopause. The Catholic Italian mother who brought in her sixteen-year-old daughter and sobbed with relief afterward. The women who were always careful with birth control, and the ones who weren't. Occasionally a woman comes in and says she's flat-out opposed to abortion but wants one anyway.

"It's still a woman's biggest secret," says Sally. "Whenever I tell someone where I work, the stories come out of the closet." Her own grandmother had a secret abortion in 1925. Afterward, she had to have a total hysterectomy. "Elderly women say, thank God for people like you."

The secret is still big—so big that some women don't tell their husbands or boyfriends. "They get the post-op instructions, and some will just tip them in the garbage on the way home," says Sally. They're wary of men who pressure a woman to have a baby when she's unwilling. They tell her, "This is your life." If she needs to pretend she had a miscarriage, they tell her what to say.

They see plenty of women from other cultures: women who've tried to use the rhythm method because they've been told the Pill is wrong; women whose husbands refuse to use condoms; women who haven't learned how to stand up for themselves.

"We tell them, 'You're living in Canada now,'" says Sally. "'Try to be strong. Take a stand here. You shouldn't have to go through this.'"

Abortion is as old as pregnancy itself. "Women throughout history have always had ways and means to terminate unintended pregnancies," says Jan. Women have also abandoned babies they couldn't provide for, or sent them off to institutions to die. The nurturing gene, despite the way we sentimentalize, romanticize, politicize or canonize it, is always tempered by reality and by nature.

But why do the reproductive wars still rage so fiercely, thirty years after we legalized abortion and fifty years after we invented the Pill? If we've long ago thrown open the door to women's reproductive self-determination, why do so many people want to slam it back shut?

I think the answer is that people in every culture have always battled over reproductive issues, and probably always will.

Sarah Blaffer Hrdy, the brilliant anthropologist, writes in her book *Mother Nature*, "Passionate debates about abortion derive from motivations to control female reproduction that are far older than any particular system of government, older than patriarchy, older even than recorded history. Male fascination with the reproductive affairs of female group members predates our species."

Barb, Sally and Jan all have kids of their own. They struck me as warm, nurturing, extremely competent and hard-headed. They're sick of Michael Coren and Dr. Laura and the strident voices that seem to dominate the airwaves. They think that calling the morning-after pill "human pesticide" (and calling people such as themselves baby-killers) fuels the inflammatory climate that sets off the crazies. But they're not particularly fearful for their own safety. "You can't do your job if you're afraid," says Jan.

I think of women's remarkably long reproductive lives (a by-product of progress) and all the chances we have to get pregnant—four or five hundred in a lifetime. I think of the pregnancy scares I had when I was single. They're a deeply private and inescapable part of every woman's experience, no matter how prudent she is. I think of all the secrets that women still don't tell.

The guy on the radio just doesn't get it. But why should he? "All high-status male primates are intent on controlling when, where and how females belonging to their group reproduce," writes Dr. Hrdy. In other words, it's just his nature.

What Will the World Do Without My Mom?

My mother, although she hates my saying so, is the answer to a right-wing politician's prayers. She is a good neighbour and a kind person, and she likes to help other people. She does the grocery shopping for the little old lady next door and takes the lady's cat to the vet. When a friend of hers came down with cancer, she took her to the doctor and helped her buy a wig.

When the single woman down the street slipped on the ice and broke her arm in three places, it was my mother who phoned 911. When the neighbour's arm was in a cast, my mother made her meals and took them over. She also figured out how to file an insurance claim so that the neighbour could get paid for the three months she was off work.

Mom's a one-woman voluntary social services agency—a combination of Wheeltrans, Meals-on-Wheels, social worker, community advocate, grief counsellor and financial adviser. Without her, the people she helps out would find it a lot harder to get by.

All of this is classic women's work—the kind of simple, generous, time-consuming neighbourliness that is essential to strong and healthy human communities. If Stephen Harper could clone my mom and put her on every block, many wrenching questions we face over how to look after kids and old folks and people in trouble would disappear.

Unfortunately, women like my mother are in short supply. The women who used to do so much unpaid elder care, sick care and childminding aren't available anymore. They've got jobs, and don't have the time.

We've replaced caregiving that used to be informal and free (and that some people never got at all) with caregiving that's institutional, expensive and theoretically available to everyone. We've democratized, professionalized and monetized it, and paid for it with higher taxes. We've replaced babysitting (done on a swap basis, or by teenagers at fifty cents an hour) with daycare and prekindergarten and after-school programs, delivered by higher-paid women with credentials, in buildings that have to meet safety standards and fire codes. We've built women's shelters so that battered wives have somewhere to go other than back home to Mom and Dad. Great-grandma lived at home till she died, tended by a dutiful daughter, but Grandma lives in a long-term care facility at $160 a day.

But the need for women's work is growing. Old people live much longer, go in and out of hospital more and may not have relatives nearby to help them out. Big cities are full of young mothers, many of them from different cultures, who may have poor parenting skills and few social supports. They and their kids are our most vulnerable citizens, and we don't have a very good idea how to help them out.

We're wonderful at managing matters of life and death—the big stuff. It's the little stuff that's falling through the cracks. In the name of efficiency, we move a new mom through the birthing centre in eighteen hours. If she has trouble learning to breastfeed, we'll send her home with a video. Maybe someone will be there to cook and clean for her—or maybe not.

None of those small things matters very much on its own. But together, they add up to one big thing—a community that works, where people in times of need have other people to fall back on. None of us knows how to make sure those fallbacks are there, and none of us knows whether they'll be there for us.

We can't replace the work that women used to do. And without them, our world feels pretty fragile.

Chapter Seven

Kids Today

I grew up in a more carefree time. In the new suburbs of the fifties and sixties, with their rambling backyards and vacant lots, kids ran in packs from dawn till dusk, without benefit of adult supervision. If our parents worried about predators lurking in the woods, they didn't mention it to us. We walked to school by ourselves and rode our bikes helmet-free, without any idea of the dangers that could do us in at any moment. We played on swings and slides that would be condemned today, and nobody told us you could drop dead from inhaling peanut butter.

My parents adopted a laissez-faire view of their duties. So long as we didn't play in the traffic, they figured the rest of our upbringing would take care of itself. There was no such word as "parenting." A parent was something you just were, not something you did. Today, parents are faced with endless decisions and live in fear that if they choose wrong, their children could be paying the price for life. Parenting is an exhausting job that starts long before birth, when conscientious parents expose their fetus to classical music and other good influences. Shortly after birth the flashcards start. Then comes the search for the kind of daycare that's stimulating enough to help your two-year-old live up to her potential. No parent can relax for a minute. I have friends who hired a tutor for their six-year-old so that she could get into French immersion. Parents are obliged to be on the lookout for every opportunity to get their children's little neurons firing on all cylinders and give them a jump-start in the ruthless competition that is life.

At the same time, kids today have to cope with pressures we never even dreamed of. Some grow up in homes without dads. All of them grow up in a popular culture that is saturated with sex and obsessed with body image. When I was in eighth grade, I was anxious about kissing. Then I grew up and cheered on the sexual revolution. Now eighth-grade girls are anxious about blow jobs. Is this progress? I don't think so.

Despite this, our worries about the children of the middle class are preposterously overblown. Entire industries have been built on how we're ruining them and how we must reform our parenting and schooling practices to rescue them from certain disaster. And nothing stoked middle-class anxieties more than the Great Girl Panic of the nineties.

The Girls Will Be All Right

Happy birthday, Leona. I know you're working hard on pronouncing the word "three," because next week that's how old you'll be. I bought you a present. It's a video of *The Paper Bag Princess*, which is a story about a girl who can do anything she wants. I figure you're going to need it.

Anyone could forgive an anxious aunt for worrying about what life has in store for you. Danger in every shadow, bad men behind every tree, poverty and discrimination—that's what girls are in for. The moral panic over girls obsessed the media for a generation. It's a good thing you can't read yet, because if you could, you'd feel like heading right back to where you came from. You are embarked on a path of lifelong victimhood, and by the time you grow up you'll be entitled to a button saying "I am a survivor."

What's the matter with being born a girl? Just about everything. Certain so-called experts say that one in six of you (or one in four, depending on which study you prefer) will be sexually abused by the time you reach adolescence. By fourth or fifth grade, some of you will develop eating disorders. Somebody will pull the plug on your self-esteem and it will all go down the drain.

By the time you're in seventh grade you'll start to lose your voice. The boys will drown you out in class. You'll make sure you don't act too smart, and if you get nineties you'll pretend they're seventies. Later you will drop calculus (math phobia, of course), and you'll start to hate your body. Then you'll go to college and worry about date rape.

When you enter the workforce, you'll make seventy-two

cents for every dollar a man makes. You will not know how to ask for a raise. You will not get promoted as far or as fast as the men who will sexually harass you on the job. When you get married and have kids, you will collapse from stress and exhaustion as you juggle the demands of child care and work. If you work you'll feel guilty, and if you stay at home you'll feel depressed, and if you don't have kids at all you will regret it for the rest of your life.

You'll do twice as much housework as your selfish, loutish husband. But God help you if you get divorced, because you'll be doomed to a life of poverty. You will be told to fear dark streets and parking garages because so many women are attacked in public places by strangers. You will be told to fear your home because of spousal abuse. When you're fifty he'll dump you for a younger model. And then you'll get breast cancer!

Poor kid. If that's what you're in for, you'll need a lot more help than you'll get from *The Paper Bag Princess.*

Fortunately, there's another version of your future. It's not the one peddled by the newspapers, women's magazines or women's studies departments in the universities, but it's a lot more accurate. While they stayed soaked in victimology, the world changed. How much? So much that one seven-year-old girl I know asked her mother, "Mom, can boys be doctors too?" The only doctors she'd ever met were women.

Fifty years ago your grandmother wanted to be a doctor. Back then it was an either-or world for girls: marriage or med school. Marriage won. She married her high school sweetheart and had three kids, and never did become a doctor (although she became a lot of other things). You won't have to make a choice like that. In fact, today you've got a better chance of getting into med school than a man.

You belong to the first generation of girls raised to believe they can be anything they want to be. You've seen women doing every kind of work. You will be able to choose if, when and how to have a family. In school, the boys are eating your dust. In universities across North America, the women outnumber the men by three to two. Women outnumber men today in law school and med school. In fact, your main problem will be finding someone to marry who has as much education as you do.

I can't promise that you'll have it all, all at once. No one does. But you'll have more chances than any generation of girls ever had before. You'll have money, or the skills to earn it. You'll know what you're worth. And women who know their worth don't have to tolerate abuse in their lives. It's as simple as that.

For the past thirty years it has been deeply unfashionable to reveal the shockingly good news about the lives of girls. A lot of people will say I'm in denial. I'd like those people to meet the girls I know. They have never lost their voice, and they never will. Victims? Never.

Boy Trouble

So if the girls will be all right we can all relax, right? Wrong. The social scientists have locked on to a brand-new group of underdogs. The victims du jour are—you guessed it—boys.

That's right. Boys are the new girls. They are tormented by unattainable ideals and constantly assaulted by commercial images of physical perfection that drive them to strive obsessively for the right look. They hate their bodies. They are riddled with self-loathing and crippling psychological debilities. They are objectified by members of the opposite sex, who only care about appearance. Many of them live in constant fear of physical attack.

"The Troubled Life of Boys," said the cover of *The New York Times Magazine,* which devoted an entire issue to the miseries of male adolescence. There's even a male version of the evil Barbie doll. Villain Number One for boys' self-esteem turns out to be a little plastic doll called G.I. Joe, whose biceps, if life-sized, would measure an astonishing thirty-two inches.

Forget what you read in *Reviving Ophelia.* It was Hamlet who had the real problems. Books with titles like *Real Boys, Raising Cain, Wonder Boys* and *Lost Boys* are flying off the shelves. According to the experts, boys are crippled by sex-role stereotyping that channels them into a stiflingly narrow band of conventional behaviour. They are damaged by their own parents, who try to mould them to fit society's gender expectations. They are shortchanged in school by a system that favours the other sex. Their cries for help go unheard; they are silenced.

Whew. If my niece Leona had been born a boy, she'd have it even worse.

The lost-boys industry got a huge boost from the Columbine shootings in Colorado and the copycat crimes that followed, including the school shooting in Taber, Alberta. Instead of condemning these kids as rare and twisted little psychopaths, we plunged into an orgy of introspection. We were sure that something in society had produced such monsters. Experts like William Pollack (*Real Boys*) claim not to be surprised. "I think we have a national crisis of boys in America," he pronounced confidently. "It's boys who are doing this, because of this code about what they can say and can't say, how they feel about their body self, how they feel about their self-image, how they feel about themselves in school." (Personally, I think the real question raised by Columbine was how a couple of middle-class suburban kids could lay their hands on an arsenal of deadly weapons without their parents noticing.)

Some of the most sought-after experts on masculinity in crisis are, oddly, feminists. Susan Faludi's *Stiffed* explains how men "are at the mercy of social forces distorting their lives."

All of these experts paint a picture of a boy's world so bleak and cheerless, so soulless and lethal, it could come straight out of *Lord of the Flies*. The weak are endlessly bullied by the strong, beaten up, pushed around and taunted. Any sign of difference is an excuse for ostracism, and any sign of emotion or sensitivity is cruelly ridiculed. In the unforgiving hierarchy of boy culture, only the handsome jocks have status. Everyone else—nerd, geek, Goth, or plain, unlabelled loser—is subject to emotional abuse causing scars that may last a lifetime. Worst of all, they can't share their pain. The culture demands that they suppress it.

If much of this sounds eerily familiar, it is. What we have here is the pathologizing of normal adolescence—just as we had in those phenomenally popular books of a decade ago that delineated the tragedy of teenage girls. The dreary truth is that modern adolescence is an excruciating time when peer pressure reigns supreme, self-esteem vanishes, hormones rage, sex roles are exaggerated and the struggle for identity begins in earnest. So what else is new? Fortunately, it doesn't last long.

The experts propose various contradictory remedies for the malady of adolescent boyhood. Some of them say we need to encourage boys to act more like girls: to express their feelings, to openly care and share. Others think we need to help them be more like men used to be, back in the days when every man could hold a good honest job and a good honest place in family life.

Today, the hottest topic in education is how to help the boys. The remedies suggested range from more boy-friendly books (Surprise! Boys are interested in cowboys and cars) to more recess (Surprise! Boys have a hard time sitting still) and more male role models (Guess what! Boys admire hockey stars).

To the average parent, this may seem like a stunning revelation of the obvious. But in education, it's an earthquake. An entire generation of educational theory has been rooted in the notion that gender is socially constructed and that boys and girls are the same. The schools have made things worse by pathologizing normal boy behaviour. If the kid can't sit still and pay attention, he'll get a label. The school system treats boys as defective girls.

But today, it's nature, not nurture, that rules the education conferences. The experts are showing up with brain scans to prove their point that gender makes a difference after all. Some people are even crusading to bring back single-sex education, so that instructional methods can be tailored to boys and girls' very different brains. "These differences are real," one expert argues. "They are grounded in biology."

Meantime, on our doorstep is another social revolution. The girls of Leona's generation are growing up confident, goal-oriented and self-sufficient. They're used to paying their own way, and won't have to depend on men for much of anything. Who will they marry? How will they bring up their own kids? What does it mean when women are the main breadwinners and also the main nurturers? We may be about to find out.

The Sexiest Boys' Toys on the Block

The girls are all right—mostly. But adolescence is still treacherous, and in one way we adults have done a terrible job. We launched the sexual revolution, and now it has come back to bite our children in ways we never could have imagined.

Forty years ago, the Beatles went on Ed Sullivan and sang "I Want to Hold Your Hand." Dads across North America went ballistic when their darling daughters brought home boyfriends with hair down to their collars.

Today, a rap star named 50 Cent has a song that goes like this: "Baby if you get on your knees, put me in your mouth and suck me off." He was nominated for five Grammys.

Dads across North America are going ballistic when they discover that their darling daughters have joined the Rainbow Club. Never heard of it? It's when girls line up to act out the 50 Cent song with a boy, and they all have different shades of lipstick on. It's a hot topic in middle school.

Am I allowed to be shocked now?

When Janet Jackson exposed her nipple ornament on network TV, the fashionable reaction was to pooh-pooh the prudery of the official response. What's the matter with those folks? Can't they take the sight of a decorated nipple? Do they really think a flash of naked breast will corrupt the nation's youth?

Oh, how sophisticated we've all become.

Call me a member of the Morally Uptight Club if you want, but I'd argue that there's a direct connection between Janet Jackson's tit-flash and the outbreak of oral sex in middle school.

Justin Timberlake's grab at his singing partner's breast was the climax, if you'll pardon the expression, of a dance routine in which women writhed on the floor in costumes that, like Janet's, would be right at home at an S&M orgy. The halftime show also featured a hip-hop singer repeatedly grabbing at his crotch. "Bet I'll have you naked by the end of this song," sang Mr. Timberlake, as he ripped off Janet's clothing. Since when did simulated sexual assault become cute?

And if you think this display was a vulgar new low in popular culture, you haven't been paying attention. This halftime show was merely an unscheduled spillover of standard MTV fare onto a Big Three network. In case you haven't noticed, Madonna has been groping herself on stage ever since her Blonde Ambition tour. Britney Spears's sexually saturated Lolita act is so familiar it's banal. When the entire culture is telling little girls to be not only sexually precocious but hypersexed, is it any wonder that deviant behaviour is now mainstream too?

At high school dances in your neighbourhood, the girls are competing to service the quarterback. Each one hopes that if she's the most skilful, he'll like her the best. Take a look at the friends your daughter is having for a sleepover. Chances are those kids in PJs are talking about BJs.

It's so liberated of us to celebrate lesbian sex on TV. When Madonna and Britney tongue each other, we laugh because the scene is so hokey and contrived, and we figure it's so, you know, harmless. So I guess it must be harmless when the guys at school egg on the girls to tongue-kiss each other while they watch. I mean, they're not serious either.

How did popular culture become so degraded? Well, we were the liberated generation, weren't we? We were going to be more relaxed and free about these matters. We weren't going to impose our parents' stupid hang-ups about sex onto our own kids. We weren't going to get all uptight over their perfectly natural sexual urges, or the chastity of our daughters. We weren't going to intrude on their privacy the way our parents did, or try to censor their music the way our parents did, or chaperone their parties and wreck their fun and lock them up in chastity belts. We would trust them, the way our parents never trusted us.

Instead of guarding our daughters' virginity, we would teach them empowerment and self-respect. Now they think empowerment means being the sexiest little boy's toy on the block. So much for a generation of feminism.

What interests me is what sort of behaviour we're willing to tolerate and what we aren't. Twelve-year-old girls who dress like hookers are fine. Meantime, we think boys who wave toy guns deserve to be severely punished. We believe that violence, even of the simulated kind, is so toxic that we've got to exercise constant vigilance and zero tolerance. We believe that parents who spank their kids are guilty of child abuse. We won't even let our kids throw snowballs in the schoolyard. Meantime, those same kids are wondering if there's something wrong with them because they haven't had oral sex yet.

"Girl you know I like it when you climb on top / Love muscles feel tighter than a headlock," sings 50 Cent in a song titled "I Smell Pussy." He didn't win any Grammys this time. I suppose we should be grateful.

The Ghost Children of the North

For all the worrying and hand-wringing we like to do about our own kids, the most endangered children in Canada are also the most invisible. They are the ghost children of the North.

"I want to die the same way my brother died—by sniffing gas," says Angela Rich, age sixteen. "I won't stop sniffing gas because when I do, I can see my brother."

Angela's little brother, Charles, died when the bag of gas he was sniffing spilled near a candle and exploded. The flames tore down his throat. He was eleven.

They look like beings possessed by evil spirits, laughing vacantly at the television cameras. They come back to haunt us whenever the latest epidemic of solvent abuse or suicide breaks out. They live in Sheshatshiu, Davis Inlet, Pikangikum. The places are different; the stories are always the same.

Do we, the viewers, care? Evidently not. "What underlies this apathy?" asked a newspaper editorial. "It's racism. Not overt—maybe not even conscious, but there, appearing as a lack of empathy."

It is, indeed, racism, but not the kind we think it is. If any kid next door to you or me were as neglected and abused and damaged as these kids are, the child-protection authorities would snatch him in a second and never send him back. There would be public outrage if they did not.

But when the children are Native, saving them is not allowed. That would be construed as blaming the victims, and it's easier to blame governments. Saving them is not allowed because of the long, long shadow cast by the residential school removals. And the truth about government "indifference" is that governments don't dare intervene in band affairs.

Finally, Innu leaders in Labrador asked for help. "They are suggesting they don't want political correctness to interfere this time," said Newfoundland's minister of health. But will a new detox centre in Labrador really save Angela Rich? What about her sister, Nympha, who personally pled for help from the prime minister?

The answer is: almost certainly not.

Not long ago, I spoke with a woman who taught school for several years in Pikangikum, an Ojibway settlement of 1,700 people located three hundred kilometres northeast of Thunder Bay. There's a suicide epidemic there.

"The first year I taught there, there were four suicides in one week," she recalls. Alcohol is banned on the reserve, but people brew their own alcohol and at least 125 kids sniff gas. After three generations of substance abuse, a significant number of children and adults suffer from fetal alcohol syndrome, which causes cognitive impairment, poor impulse control and other lasting damage. Child neglect and child sexual abuse are common, and kids roam free. Literacy rates are low. Band leaders are poorly educated and the place is torn apart by band politics. Girls get pregnant at thirteen or fourteen. Worst of all, there's nothing to do.

When asked about their biggest problems, Native kids always mention boredom. The boredom of lives without goals or purpose or role models. Chronic, toxic, deadly boredom.

In Toronto and Vancouver, troubled teenage girls get anorexia. In Pikangikum, they form suicide pacts. The social workers call them "cluster suicides." Imagine if two thousand kids committed suicide in Toronto this year. That's equivalent to the suicide rate in the Pikangikum area.

It's true that the majority culture (that's us) bears some responsibility for these things. But chewing over old wrongs won't help the children now. Nor will nostalgia for the old days of hunting and gathering. The Innu have snowmobiles, and the old days are never coming back.

There are already treatment centres for Native kids. One is in London, Ontario, and lots of kids there are Innu. The counsellors detoxify them and teach them life skills and coping skills and are sensitive to Native traditions. The kids go to Raptors games and Canada's Wonderland. The treatment works extremely well—until they send the kids back.

And yet we still pretend that new detox centres, new recreation centres, new houses, parenting-skills courses, healing rituals, more social workers and fantasies about attracting the tourist trade can somehow make up for the lack of purpose in places where there is no work and nothing meaningful to do.

When we talk about the troubles of urban ghettos, we do everything we can to help the kids get an education and get out to seek a better life. Yet the Native ghettos of the North are places we do everything we can to make sure the children never leave. At least in urban ghettos of the south, the kids aren't totally cut off from the world. Yet we think it's a good idea to isolate the poorest kids of all hundreds of kilometres away from first-rate schools and art and commerce, from the world of achievement and success. That is our national policy.

How arrogant we are, how naive and how cruel. And how long, in the name of self-determination and good intentions, will we repeat the cycle of abuse?

Dreams of Martyrdom

After 9/11, I realized that the way other cultures raise their children matters just as much to us as how we raise our own. That's how I found myself in a Palestinian town in the West Bank. I had gone to meet the parents of a vibrant and beautiful eighteen-year-old girl named Ayat Akras. I hoped that they could help me understand why their daughter had chosen to blow herself up.

On a March day in 2002, Ayat slipped across the border to Israel and took a cab to a supermarket on the edge of Jerusalem. She had explosives around her waist and a powerful bomb in her handbag. The store was crowded with people shopping for the Sabbath, and her mission was to kill as many of them as possible. As she tried to go in the door, the guard sensed something was wrong and tried to stop her. That's when she detonated herself. She killed him, and herself, and injured more than twenty other people. She also killed an Israeli girl named Rachel Levy. Rachel was seventeen. They looked so alike that they could have been sisters.

I spoke to Ayat's parents in the living room of their tiny two-room concrete house. As in other Arab houses, the sofas were arranged neatly around the walls. We sipped sweet strong tea as we talked.

Ayat didn't fit the standard profile of a terrorist. She had never held a weapon or shouted "Death to Israel." She did not belong to Hamas or Islamic Jihad. She was just a schoolgirl, with long black hair and dark brown eyes, a straight-A average and a fiancé. Her father told me proudly about her top marks in school, and she had made her fiancé promise that she could go to university.

A quiet girl, Ayat had become increasingly angry at the violence and unrest. One day Israeli soldiers killed a neighbour across the street. "She was terribly upset," her mother told me. But her mother didn't approve of suicide bombing. They used to watch the news together on TV where suicide bombers were glorified. "I said, 'It's none of your business and none of mine. It's your business to finish your studies and get married.'" She had no idea her daughter had gotten to know the militants in the town and had volunteered for a suicide mission.

Before the Israelis closed the border in an effort to stop the bombers, Ayat's father had worked as a foreman building Jewish houses. He had made friends with many Jews. "Politics is one thing, and work is something else," he told me. "We would work together, eat together, live together, like family." As for his own family, he said, "I taught my children to love life."

Her mother told me she was angry at the men who had recruited her daughter for a suicide mission. She said she grieved for the family of the Israeli girl Ayat had killed. But the family was also proud of their martyred daughter, and they had turned the living room into a sort of shrine to her. A framed certificate of academic excellence hung on a wall. On another wall was a poster-sized photograph with a traditional religious exhortation stitched in needlepoint. "God urges the believers to perform jihad against the enemy," it read in Arabic.

Another photo is the studio shot that most suicide bombers have taken before they blow themselves up. It shows Ayat in a *kaffiyeh,* the checked headdress. She looks fierce, and in her arms she cradles a gun. There's another photo too. It shows another side of Ayat—a thoroughly modern young woman, dressed in flared blue jeans, her long brown hair uncovered, posed saucily against a backdrop of the Manhattan skyline.

Those two photos summed up Ayat's choice: the old world or the new. The medieval or the modern. The cult of death or the culture of life. She chose death. Why, when she could have had the other?

In Ayat's world, the message of the media is that death is glorious.

In Palestine, the music videos on TV star attractive boys and girls in Western fashions and are set to catchy music. But they're not about sex and love. They're about death. Among the most common themes is the wickedness and depravity of the enemy—the Israelis. Another theme is the beauty of *shahada—*

dying for Allah—which is depicted as the supreme act of patriotism. Boyfriends and girlfriends are shown reunited in Heaven after they blow themselves up.

The news and talk shows carry the same message. On one talk show, two bright, well-spoken eleven-year-old girls expressed their longing for martyrdom. They talked about growing up to be martyrs the same way girls in Canada talk about growing up to be teachers or doctors or brides. "*Shahada* is very, very beautiful," said a girl named Walla. "Everyone yearns for *shahada*. What could be better than going to Paradise?"

"What is better," asked the host, "peace and full rights for the Palestinian people, or *shahada*?"

"*Shahada*. I will achieve my rights after becoming a *shahida*," the little girl answered.

A few weeks after Ayat's death, the director of the Palestinian children's aid association explained in a television interview that part of education policy is to teach children to aspire to death for Allah. "The concept of *shahada* for him [the child] means belonging to the homeland, from a religious point of view. Sacrifice for his homeland. Achieving *shahada* in order to reach Paradise and to meet his God. This is the best."

Ayat's heroic death is admired by all her friends. But what about the innocent people she killed? "Oh no," one of them told me. "She is not a murderer. After you see what we've seen, all of us want to do what she did. But I don't have her courage."

The girls in Ayat's neighbourhood are very modern. They dress fashionably, mixing pieces of East and West—flared jeans, stylish boots and hijab. And they discuss martyrdom the way Western girls discuss weddings.

"It's sensational, it's awesome, it makes me think anyone would love to be in her place," said a fourteen-year-old named Shireen. Shireen is very good at math. She says that if she can't be a martyr, she'll settle for being a doctor.

Ayat went to high school a few kilometres away, in a large, modern, airy building with a spectacular view of the hills around Jerusalem. On a wall in front of the school, I saw a little painting of a dove of peace. Just inside the front door, there was a giant mural of Ayat. It was a copy of the photo that showed her in her martyr's pose with a gun. Inside, I met the principal, a pleasant, welcoming woman in a skirt and sweater. "Every person in our society considers her a hero," the principal told me.

As I sipped tea with Ayat's parents in their house, several of their granddaughters came in to play. One adorable little girl of eight or so was playing with a pink plastic gun. Among the children, *shahid* games are very popular now.

Chapter Eight

Schools 'R' Us

I was fourteen the year I decided to disguise my brain. I was enrolled in Grade 10, in a typical Canadian high school in a middle-income suburb of Toronto. It was a vast intellectual wasteland. Browners, as they were known, were somewhere near the bottom of the pecking order. Browners were students who studied too hard. Like unionized garbage collectors who pick up trash too fast, they were thought to spoil things for everybody else.

Even greasers from the dummy classes were more popular than browners. So I took up smoking cigarettes with the greasers behind the shopping plaza. I lied about my marks and pretended not to study, which was not hard because the classes were so easy I didn't have to.

Modern public high schools are the most dysfunctional institutions yet devised by the developed world. They deaden the souls, confine the bodies and bludgeon the spirits of the inmates. They incarcerate young people in their prime and trap them into the cruel hierarchies of adolescent society. Their intellectual climate is unspeakably banal, and their life lessons are all wrong. They are a breeding ground for every kind of teenage pathology, from bullying to bulimia. They're bad for girls, and even worse for boys.

The kids who trash the buildings every so often "aren't necessarily politically conscious," one eighteen-year-old told me. "They just hate the place."

I did too.

"From the schools' point of view, they have thousands of adolescents who must be controlled and kept like barn animals," says Judith Kleinfeld, an expert on schools and adolescence. The fifty-minute bells, the homework checks and the hall passes are all essential means of crowd control. These practices are more or less guaranteed to breed contempt for authority. "The lock-step atmosphere irritates adolescents whose psychological task is to establish independent identities," she says.

Big high schools were invented in the industrial age. Maybe that's why they look so much like factories. Unlike every other institution, they've scarcely changed since. They were perfected in the 1950s, when the pedagogic wisdom was that bigger would surely be better.

As the tiny rural schools closed down, high schools bulked up to 1,000 or 2,000 kids or more. Teachers specialized, and class sizes grew, and school boards hired more and more janitors and support staff to keep the plant maintained. Principals morphed into personnel directors and safety wardens. The age of mass production had arrived.

"High school teachers want to do a good job, but they really can't with five classes of thirty kids," says Dr. Kleinfeld. "They can't possibly grade that many long essays a week. So the kids don't work, and the teachers don't make them. It's an intellectual bargain with the devil."

And it endures for years. We keep kids in school far past the age when they're ready for autonomy, spooning them full of the innocuous, inoffensive, unchallenging material that constitutes most of the high school curriculum. The best thing you can say for high schools is that they keep the inmates off the streets.

Educators pay lip service to the importance of stimulating creativity, which, we're told, is the key to succeeding in the world these days. But there's not much creativity in a factory. We need to blow up the high schools and make them small and intimate again. We need to make them places where teachers actually know who the kids are and have the time to teach them deeply.

But intellectual development is not what most Canadians really want from their school system. And if the public schools were suddenly to demand it (don't worry, they won't), parents as well as students would undoubtedly revolt.

"For a sizable number of children—and adults—reading, writing and arithmetic, to say nothing of history, geography and, above all, science, are unpleasant chores they'd just as soon avoid," says Michiel Horn, the well-known professor of Canadian history. This is demonstrably true. Eight million adult Canadians can barely read or count, and millions more can scarcely make it through a newspaper. Many of them hated school and couldn't wait to get it over with. It's unlikely they'll instill a love of learning in their children.

Whenever Canadians are asked about the most important purpose of our education system, they put "intellectual development" way down the list. The first thing we want our schools to do is to prepare the kids to get a job. The second is to turn kids into "good citizens," whatever that is. Intellectual development typically runs a poor third. This has been the case in every opinion survey ever taken.

It's conventional wisdom that a good job now requires a post-secondary degree. And so the education market has obliged—not by raising students' levels of accomplishment, but by massively expanding our post-secondary system. Anyone who wants to go to college can find somewhere to get in. It won't demand too much of them, but it will give them a credential, which is really all they want.

Ever since the Canadian historian Hilda Neatby wrote *So Little for the Mind* in 1953, the highbrows have been blasting away at our lowbrow education system. "It is frankly anti-intellectual," she wrote. "There is no attempt to exercise, train and discipline the mind."

Secondary schools were invented in nineteenth-century Prussia, in order to ensure a good supply of low-level functionaries and bureaucrats for a modern, technocratic state. In North America, the progressivists have been in charge of public education from the start. They never did believe that intellectual engagement was its main purpose.

The ideal teacher, wrote U.S. educator John Dewey, is "a social servant set apart for the maintenance of proper social order and the securing of the right social growth." In Canada, Egerton Ryerson appealed for the support of the well-to-do by arguing that universal public education would produce law-abiding citizens who would be less likely to attack their property.

It's no accident that the main purpose of so many schools appears to be to teach kids to work and play well with others. Even when parents send their kids to private school, it's not always academic excellence that's foremost in their minds. Private school provides a means of social climbing. It offers the chance for little Lauren and little Ryan to rub elbows with a better class of kid.

The education reforms that governments are trying to put in place are only incidentally, if at all, about academic excellence. Why must we raise standards? Not to instill a love of learning or teach the habits of skeptical inquiry. Canadians are far more pragmatic than that. We must raise standards so that kids are better trained for the workplace.

"If public schools manage to turn out kids who are more tolerant and less violent than they were in the past while also teaching some intellectual content, maybe they're doing about all that can be reasonably expected," says Professor Horn.

As for me, my mother yanked me from behind the shopping plaza and sent me (at ruinous expense) to a girls' school. It didn't stop me smoking on the sly, but at least it was the kind of place where I didn't have to hide the fact that I liked to read. It was one of those schools that people sneer at as "elitist."

We like to rant and rave about our public education system. But it's entirely possible that (except for all the strikes) the one we have is more or less the one we want.

Who Has Seen the Teacher?

In the mid-1930s, my husband's aunt, Margaret McLeod, got her first teaching job in a one-room school outside Megantic, Quebec. She had sixteen or eighteen pupils of all ages. She was in her early twenties and had only a high school education, but she was smart. She'd won first place in the provincial final exams for students outside of Montreal.

Like other rural teachers, Margaret lived with the family of one of her students. Her pay was room and board and a few hundred dollars a year.

Back then, teaching was just about the only profession open to a bright young woman. I doubt that Margaret would choose to be a teacher now. Today, she'd probably go to law school or become a scientist.

And who would blame her? Teaching is a less and less appealing line of work. The system is in chaos. The work is hard (if you do it well), and the pay, while considerably better than it was in Margaret's day, has been slipping for a decade.

Margaret's social standing was relatively high. People looked up to her. Today, teachers get more pity than respect. And thousands of them across the country are packing in their chalk for good. The schools are desperately short of people who can teach the hard sciences, technical studies, math and French. They're desperately short of men to teach in middle and elementary school. The men are too worried they'll be accused of sexual abuse.

A massive teaching shortage has struck the Western world. Supply and demand are seriously out of whack, but union wage rules and caps on education budgets mean the market can't correct itself. Even if a school board had the money to pay a high school physics teacher more than a Grade 2 teacher, it's not allowed to. So few people are interested in these teaching specialities that faculties of education are cancelling classes for lack of enrolment.

As teaching's appeal has declined, so has the quality of new teachers. No one will say so outright. But a decade ago, there were four applicants for every space in faculties of education. Today, in Ontario, the ratio is less than two to one. A lot of people go to teachers' college because their marks aren't good enough to get into something else.

Many U.S. school boards have larded on the goodies to get new teachers. Their recruiting teams have become familiar sights in Canada. Some places offer moving expenses, signing bonuses and car allowances, even differential salaries in areas where they're short. They recruit science teachers from places such as Poland for two- or three-year assignments. And they're trying various fast-track schemes to lure mid-career people from other fields.

Canada, as usual, is far less market-oriented. Are you a chemist looking for a mid-life career change? Let's hope you're independently well off. Most school boards won't pay you a bean for your other work experience. How does $35,000 sound to start?

Having said all that, I've met plenty of outstanding educators. They work harder for less money than anyone I know. They're the unsung heroes of the system, and I admire them more than anyone I know.

"He Is Our Teacher"

It's a sweaty, muggy summer afternoon, and Johnnie Williams is preaching to a tough crowd—a group of inner-city boys, almost all of them black. They don't look all that happy to be here. No wonder. It's a school, their least favourite place on earth.

"You cannot be successful if you have no enthusiasm!" he tells them, moving energetically back and forth across the front of the room. He grabs a basketball to illustrate a point. "You can't play if there's no air inside the ball. And you can't play the game of life without something inside your head."

These kids are used to getting D's and F's. To them, school is a form of temporary incarceration. But Johnnie is a draw. As the brother of a genuine basketball celebrity (Jerome Williams, a.k.a. the Raptors' former Junk Yard Dog), he commands a certain credibility. As a former pro basketball player himself (he was grounded by an injury), he gets respect.

"We're here to pass on information," he says. "And when the ball gets passed to you, I want you to stand up and say in one word what a man is."

He throws the ball to a kid in the third row. The kid stands up and mumbles, "responsibility."

Johnnie's pep talk uses basketball as a metaphor for the game of life. It's part of an intensive program to show these kids what it takes to succeed. Around the room are other adult mentors who have volunteered their time to shoot hoops with the kids, take them to sporting events and supply informal coaching on the game of life. Many are teachers or principals in the Toronto school system, and all of them are black. One of the principals wears his hair in dreads, tied up in a ponytail. If principals are allowed to look like this, the school system is definitely doing something right.

But this program wasn't started by a bureaucrat. It's the brainchild of Chris Spence, a remarkable educator who is now, lucky for us, a school superintendent. He's an education entrepreneur, a passionate, committed leader determined to make a difference. The program he founded is called Boys to Men, and it's about values, not just education. Its most important message is what it means to be a man. And the three key words are Pride, Dignity, Respect.

"Can you make that personal commitment to figure out what those words mean?" Johnnie asks the crowd. "Yeah," they say, a bit half-heartedly. It's only their second session. But afterward, they crowd enthusiastically around the adults.

For black boys this age—Grade 6 on up through high school—the peer pressure to drop out and do drugs and crime is overwhelming. Their only models of successful manhood are rap singers and basketball stars, and their teacher may be the only black man they've ever met who has been to college.

"Be the leader, don't follow the majority," says a line in the rap song that's played at the beginning and end of every session. "Don't rob yourself of your own destiny."

Before this program, some of these kids had never been out of their own neighbourhoods. Far too many of them believe they'll never live anywhere else. And in this world, doing well in school attracts suspicion, not respect.

"People say, 'You're selling out,'" says Andre Patterson, the school principal with the dreadlocks. "But I say, 'You're negotiating the system.'"

The other message the kids get drummed into them is that they will not wind up in the NBA. "The first thing black males identify with is their athletic ability," says Mr. Patterson. "We have to break down that image. The fact is that they have a better chance of becoming a doctor or lawyer than an NBA player. We need more mentors to come out and say it and do something about it."

Chris Spence always knew he wanted to teach in what are known as "special-needs" schools. When he walked into his first classroom, he recalls, the kids could scarcely believe their eyes. "I told you, I told you . . . He is black and he is our teacher," they marvelled. The kids were in middle school, but some of them could barely write their names. He and some of the other teachers were deeply dismayed. They also were unwilling to settle for the status quo. "I never made peace with the fact that these kids were almost out of the race of life at such an early age because they lacked an education," he writes in his recently published school memoir. (It's called *On Time! On Task! On a Mission!*) "Our response to this was to have school on Saturdays, during vacations, and at night to make up the difference—whatever it takes."

This was the start of Boys to Men, a program that has now expanded to two dozen schools. No bureaucrat dreamed it up. No one waited for a government grant to get it going. It's entirely a grassroots movement, and Chris Spence believes that's its strength.

It takes more than extra classes to rescue kids like these. It takes deep caring, and also, in a world where the institutions of church and family have disintegrated, what Mr. Spence calls "moral courage."

In 1998, Mr. Spence became principal of Lawrence Heights Middle School, one of Toronto's worst-performing schools. Drug dealers, gangs and gunfire were features of the neighbourhood, and absenteeism and violence were features of the school. He set out to demand discipline and standards, raise expectations and redefine success. From now on, he declared, the school would honour academic achievement the same way it honoured its sports teams. "We beat this school by forty points in basketball and they beat us by the same score in math," he told the kids one day. "Who's going to be whose boss?"

By the spring of 2000, school morale had soared and discipline problems had all but vanished. The kids at Lawrence Heights were scoring better than the provincial average, and there was a waiting list to teach there.

Today Mr. Spence is a school superintendent. He utterly rejects the notion that inner-city kids (who, in Toronto, often live in the outer city) are doomed to fail. He believes that the real test of an education system is how well it educates the least well off.

By that measure, our education system is a dismal failure.

But it doesn't have to be. He's shown the way. More money for education would, no doubt, be helpful. But what the system really needs is more people with moral courage like Chris Spence.

Chapter Nine

Our Royals

America has Hollywood celebrities and the Kennedys (even though a lot of them are dead). England has Princess Di. She is defunct too, but she and Jackie still sell more magazines than anyone. So who does Canada have?

We have celebrity envy.

Let's face facts. We're a nation of relative nobodies. After Celine, Avril and Shania, it's hard to find a face that most of us would recognize on a magazine cover (and I'm not so sure about Avril). Canada's quintessential celebrities are people like Michael J. Fox and Wayne Gretzky—really nice guys with wholesome family lives who've moved to the States.

Fortunately, we have the royals, even though we're dubious about them. We like the trappings of the monarchy, but just beneath the surface we're rabidly republican. Royals are all right with us, so long as they act as if they're nothing special. We feel the same about the very rich. God help them when they're flashy and ostentatious and carry on as if they're smarter, better-looking and more talented than we are (especially if it's true).

Our idea of an admirable billionaire is Ken Thomson, who lives among us in obscurity. He walks dogs for the Humane Society. He shops for specials in the supermarket and never carries on in public about national affairs or foreign policy. He is modest and unassuming and pinches pennies to a fault. I once found myself chatting to Mrs. Thomson at a large banquet. We agreed that the cost of living in London is absolutely shocking these days. She told me they don't spend much time there anymore because it's gotten so expensive. For a moment, I forgot I was talking to the wife of Canada's richest man.

My personal list of royal favourites is highly idiosyncratic. I admire Hilary Weston, the former lieutenant-governor of Ontario. Despite her stupendous disadvantages of great wealth, famous friends, fabulous houses, natural beauty and a handsome husband, she is a splendid, unaffected person.

Her Excellency Adrienne Clarkson is another matter. Although she works hard at her job, she has an unfortunate tendency to confuse herself with the real queen. Her consort, who has been known to travel with his own equerry, seems similarly confused. Back in Ms. Clarkson's television days, when she jetted round the world as a celebrity journalist, the TV crews all knew which stars would help them lug around the bulky camera gear and which ones wouldn't. They called it "carrying the sticks." She didn't.

But Canada's most fascinating aristocratic couple are Conrad, Lord Black of Crossharbour, and Lady Barbara. Their story is a fabulous morality tale, about great talent and ambition sabotaged by greed and arrogance. There are half a dozen biographies in the works about the Blacks, but I think only a great novelist could really do them justice. Their tale deserves the genius of a Thackeray or Trollope or perhaps Tom Wolfe.

The Lord and Lady Fade to Black

In June of 2003, Lord and Lady Black were among the guests at Hilary Weston's splendid sixtieth birthday party. The setting was Fort Belvedere, the Georgian folly of a country house the Westons rent from the Queen. (Edward VIII made it his home until 1936 when he abdicated for the woman he loved.) The Queen and Prince Philip, Queen Noor of Jordan and Princess Caroline of Monaco were there. So were many of Hilary Weston's Canadian friends, not all of whom are rich or titled. After dinner, Bryan Ferry played Hilary's favourite song and a fireworks display the royals might envy lit up the sky over Windsor Great Park.

But nobody looked more regal than Lady Black. That night she had on a gorgeous couture gown and her aristocratic air, the one that said she knew she was both rich and thin (although, as Mrs. Simpson said, you can never be too much of either one.) And when her old friends from Toronto said hello, she looked right through them, as if they were invisible, then turned away to seek out someone more important. "She had this vague, aristocratic look on her face that said, 'Now, remind me who you are again,'" says someone who was there. As one of her former friends concluded, "We are her past."

I last saw the Blacks perhaps ten years ago, shortly after they were married. A friend of mine took me along to lunch with them at a restaurant in Toronto. Barbara looked exquisite in a chic French suit and complained bitterly about how disliked she was in Canada. She had recently acquired a refined English accent. Both Blacks complained about how petty and small-minded Canadians are. After lunch, they got into their chauffeur-driven limousine and drove away.

The story of their courtship is now a legend. Conrad was besotted with Barbara from the start. And Barbara, a serial bride (Mr. Black was her fourth husband), seemed to be waiting for a man like him to come along and fulfill her destiny.

"It is about time we dismissed those ugly words of criticism (like 'meal ticket' and 'gold digger') that accompany a good marriage," she wrote more than two decades ago in *Chatelaine*. The article was called "Why Women Marry Up." "It is what society has always expected a woman to do." She opined that every woman should marry a man who makes at least twice as much as she does. That was some time during her third marriage, to a charming, handsome cable entrepreneur who was also rich, though not quite as rich as Mr. Black.

And yet it wasn't simply Conrad's money that she liked. "He understands power," she once wrote about him, when he was still married to Wife Number One. "Power is sexy, not simply in its own right, but because it inspires self-confidence in its owner and a shiver of subservience on the part of those who approach it."

At lunch that day in Toronto, it was obvious they were perfectly delighted with each other. They were just beginning their dazzling social ascent. Mr. Black, who had recently bought *The Telegraph,* was Margaret Thatcher's favourite press baron. Mrs. Black, who had made her own dazzling career in London, was introducing him to everyone who mattered. His power and money, her beauty and their combined brains made them a hit.

Back home, in the backwater of Canada, Mr. Black had failed to get *The Globe and Mail,* the prize he'd always wanted most. So he launched the *National Post,* a mouthpiece for his deeply held Thatcherite beliefs. As a business, the *Post* was a disaster. But it was the best thing that could have happened to *The Globe and Mail.* The *Globe*'s owners were forced to invest millions to improve the paper, and *Globe* readers have Conrad Black to thank for that.

Lord Black's business affairs were tortuous, to say the least. He ran them through a string of holding companies he controlled. He paid himself and his wife extravagantly. He attracted celebrity directors to his boards, and wined and dined them with the best of everything. They were richly entertained by his amusing style, his polysyllabic erudition and his unvarnished arrogance, and they never raised a peep about the way he ran the business. As for the shareholders, Lord Black treated them like pesky, whining nuisances. So were the journalists who tried to poke into his affairs. He regarded them as leftist agitators, and threatened them with lawsuits.

Meantime, the lord and lady were broadening their social horizons. They set up house in New York and Palm Beach, and began consorting with the super-duper rich. They were not discreet about it. "I have an extravagance that knows no bounds," Barbara declared to *Vogue,* which gave her a six-page photo spread and featured a tour of her extensive wardrobe. She posed in a strapless, ruched Ming-blue taffeta Oscar de la Renta ballgown ($11,000). She posed in Gaultier. She posed in a Carolina Herrera rose print blouse with sable cuffs. "I'm always worried about cleavage," she confessed naughtily. "I keep saying 'higher,' but I seem to keep spilling out of things." Mrs. Black takes pleasure in displaying her splendid assets and ignores the snickers of those discarded friends who knew her when she was flat-chested.

There is speculation that his wife's extravagance that knows no bounds may have punched a rather large hole in the Blacks' personal cash flow. At the very least, it made the shareholders hopping mad. As the criticism mounted over how her husband was running the company, she wrote an article in a glossy magazine about the burden of owning diamonds, especially a certain "fantastic natural-pearl and diamond brooch" she owns. Having to learn about diamonds, she confided, is one of the burdens of life among the upper classes. And this particular set of diamonds, she mourned, languishes in her safety deposit box because it's simply too big to wear.

There's a certain self-destructive streak to this couple that makes them irresistible. "Greed is a motive that has not failed to move me," Mr. Black once said, a touch too candidly. The conspicuous consumption was also on display in the 17,000-square-foot Palm Beach house with an elevator and a tunnel to a private beach. It was on display in the private jets—two of them because, as Barbara once explained, you never know what continent you'll be stranded on. The Blacks were millionaires who aspired to live like billionaires. Only a few hundred women in the world could afford to dress like Mrs. Black, and it's possible that Mrs. Black was not among them.

Canadians dislike vulgar display. We like everybody to be equal, or at least to act that way. And so, when Lord and Lady Black showed up at a costume ball dressed as Cardinal Richelieu and Marie Antoinette, we howled with derision. We didn't like the way that Conrad criticized and then abandoned his homeland either. We thought his lust for foreign titles was pompous and absurd. And so, when the tumbrels started rolling for the Blacks, the rabble couldn't get enough of it.

Conrad's downfall came at the hands of a straitlaced investment fund, which had bought shares in his company and began questioning some of his more dubious business practices. Soon the whole world knew about the lucrative fees he paid to himself, in return for not competing with himself, and how he'd sold off his own newspapers for a dollar to another company in which he had invested. His loyal board of directors quit or turned against him, and he was forced out as CEO. Now he has begun the next phase of his career, which will consist of fighting lawsuits well into his old age.

One of the lawsuits was launched by the directors of Hollinger International, the company he once controlled. It claimed $1.25 billion in damages and alleged that the Blacks took money from the company in a "continuing effort" to "improperly enrich themselves." The lawsuit claimed that Mr. Black had charged off the cost of refurbishing a 1958 Rolls-Royce Silver Wraith "apparently so that [they] could travel London in style without paying for the ride." It alleged that they had taken the company jet on a holiday to Bora Bora and billed the company for the costs of "chefs, senior butlers, butlers, underbutlers, housemen, footmen and security personnel." What's more, the lawsuit said Barbara tipped the doorman at Bergdorf's fifty dollars—and charged it to the company.

The media in three countries feasted on the Blacks' notorious excesses. *The Wall Street Journal* ran an exposé of his shady business dealings. *The New York Times* ran an especially snarly picture of him on its front page. And its most popular columnist, Paul Krugman, called him the leading villain of the new gilded age.

True to form, Mr. Black did not go down without a fight. He claimed that he is a victim of malicious forces conspiring against him. And he belligerently denied that his decision to sell the palace in Palm Beach meant he'd fallen on hard times. "I made fifty million bucks yesterday," he snarled to a mob of reporters the day after he was forced to step down as Hollinger CEO.

"It's odd how fast grandeur becomes gloomy when the miasma of misfortune sets in," wrote Tina Brown, the chronicler of Manhattan's elite. At the height of the scandal, Mr. Black's monumental biography of Franklin Roosevelt was published. The launch party at New York's Four Seasons was supposed to be a dazzling gathering of luminaries. Instead, it was a bust. Despite widespread acclaim for the book, only the hardiest of loyalists (including a creaky Henry Kissinger) showed up. Ms. Brown called the event "a wake for a reputation." To top it off, *The New York Times* trashed his book. "It gives off the familiar air of vanity publishing," the book reviewer sneered.

Friends tend to keep a distance when they read the papers and see words like "looting" adjacent to your name. They no longer beg for the pleasure of your company or hang on your every word. One New York socialite confessed she wished she hadn't committed to throwing him a book party. "What can we do?" she said. "We didn't know he was so greedy."

And now the Blacks' brilliant social career is over. In one of the many lawsuits Lord Black has filed against his detractors, he claims that the unfair accusations hurled his way have made people treat him like "a loathsome leper."

The Blacks are among the most gifted couples Canada has ever produced. But the problem with being rich and powerful is that no one ever reins you in. "His arrogance was charming," says Hal Jackman, who is a former friend, "but it outwore its welcome."

As for Mrs. Black, I wonder if she regrets snubbing her old friends.

Someday she might need them.

Their Excellencies Get Grounded

John Ralston Saul once called Conrad Black a maddened corgi. Mr. Saul may be the only person alive who can stand up to Mr. Black in a good slanging match. Mr. Black once referred to Mr. Saul as a "somewhat pitiful figure who has hovered and festered for some years on the fringes of Canadian government." Mr. Black's wife, Barbara Amiel, once accused Mr. Saul's wife, Adrienne Clarkson, of shouting, "Viva Castro." In return,

Ms. Clarkson called Mrs. Black a neo-conservative attack dog.

It's safe to say there's no love lost between these pairs. But they've got a surprising amount in common. Both couples have adopted a somewhat imperial style. Barbara doesn't mind being called Lady Black, and Mr. Saul, as the governor general's consort, adores being introduced as His Excellency. Both couples have lofty ideas about what's wrong with the world, although these ideas could scarcely be more different. The Blacks think Canada is too full of socialists like the Clarkson-Ralston Sauls, and the Clarkson-Ralston Sauls think the world is imperilled by capitalists like the Blacks. Both women like to dress distinctively. Both men like to hold forth for hours at a time. And both couples have come under heavy fire for their free-spending ways with other people's money.

In September 2003, Canada's governor general undertook a grand circumnavigation of the North, accompanied by pha-lanxes of aides and fifty-nine of Canada's finest writers, artists and vintners. It was envisaged as a sort of grand travelling salon that would strengthen our ties with Russia, Finland, Ice-land and other great northern nations.

But money scandals were afoot in Ottawa, and politicians were suddenly sensitive about raids on the public purse. Was this $1-million trip necessary? Well, maybe not. And when it turned out to have cost $5 million, I decided to investigate and find out what the taxpayers got for their money.

For their trip, Their Excellencies rented a Defence Depart-ment jet ($307,000). Their first stop was Moscow, where they were received by Vladimir Putin himself. Her Excellency pro-nounced Mr. Putin a very interesting man, although she was too diplomatic to add that he's a ruthless gangster in charge of a gangster state. One of the famous Canadian writers who went along on the trip had some of her poetry translated and published in a newspaper in Iceland.

Say this about them: Madame and His Excellency are no slackers. They worked like field hands. There were wreaths to lay at tombs of unknown soldiers, and reindeer farms to inspect. There was a visit to the Arctic Monument at Salekhard, which had been relocated especially for their visit so that it actually touched the Arctic Circle. There were state banquets to attend, and the Library of Lapland to tour. Mr. Saul kept busy hosting literary roundtables on such topics as "Isolation in Canadian and Finnish Literature." There were visits to geothermal power plants, and seminars on topics such as "The Importance of Citizenship."

Mr. Saul conducted professional wine-tasting events with Finnish and Icelandic sommeliers. His Excellency is a well-known oenophile and has made it his personal mission to spread the great news about Canadian wines in an effort to boost this promising export. So far, our annual wine exports to Iceland equal zero. But I suppose that just shows what an opportunity awaits us.

As the vice-regal couple were at pains to point out, theirs was not just another grubby trade mission. The real purpose of this trip was far more lofty. It was to explore the archetypal reality of the North, which all northern nations share. Or so I gathered from their speeches.

After coming under fire for her trip, Her Excellency vigorously defended herself. "It is rather frustrating that people don't understand that we are a northern country," she snapped. "It's something that a lot of people who have gone to the North get."

This strikes me as a novel view of Canada, where, in fact, almost everything that counts is in the south. Like it or not, Canada is inextricably linked by geography, history, trade and blood ties to the United States. Their Excellencies don't like that one bit. You get the impression that they'd like to saw right through the border and set Canada adrift into the Arctic Ocean. Failing that, they'll make sure we strengthen our ties with Iceland, which never tried to conquer anybody and is a much nicer country than that big bully to the south.

I, too, have been up north a couple of times. It's a splendid, wild, romantic place if you don't mind the muskeg and mosquitoes. But I've never thought of it as the essence of our national identity. The North is a vast and sparsely populated wilderness whose residents are heavily subsidized by vast sums of money from the south. For that matter, there are fewer indigenous Canadians living in the North than in downtown Toronto.

But you can't let the facts get in the way of a big idea. "The North is the reality of our culture," said His Excellency in a speech delivered at the Herzen State Pedagogical University of Russia, where he was receiving an honorary degree on our dime. "Its geography, its climate, its resulting attitudes towards space and isolation and imagination are fundamentally Northern. Not Western." Take that, you hegemonic imperialists to the south!

So why was it necessary to take all those eminent writers, artists, filmmakers and vintners along on the circumpolar tour? As Mr. Saul explained, "Because we must increase our own sense of the multiplicity of our cultural imagination." I'm not sure what that means, but it sounds impressive.

When summoned before Parliament to explain the bill, the governor general refused. "I am above Parliament," she explained. And then she was grounded. A second circumpolar tour was all set to go, but the public outrage was so great that she had to pull the plug. No more Defence Department jets. No more literary salons in Murmansk. Their Excellencies had been reduced to a more humble way of life. But I suppose they can take comfort in knowing that after leaving Rideau Hall, they will have a generous pension and a full-time staff of four—for life.

Why I Was So Wrong about Hilary Weston

When Hilary Weston was named lieutenant-governor of Ontario by her good friend Jean Chrétien, she was widely derided as a rich man's wife whose only claim to office was that she happened to be a charming socialite. A few journalists were snide about Her Majesty's new representative, including me.

"I would like to extend my sincere thanks to the Prime Minister for this brilliant appointment," I wrote in 1996. "Hilary Weston will be a shining example to the ordinary women of this province. And I would like to thank Mrs. Weston, in advance, for the sacrifices she is about to make in the name of duty. She will, for example, have to step aside from her beloved job as deputy chairwoman of Holt Renfrew. I just hope she can get those third-floor dressing rooms remodelled before she goes. The ones at the Bloor and Yonge store. They really are quite tacky."

Okay. I eat my words. Mrs. Weston has proved that even the privileged can have class.

Five years later, as the end of her term drew near, I spent a few hours with Her Honour. I sincerely hoped she wouldn't bring my rudeness up. Of course she didn't. She has perfect manners.

It was a big day at Toronto East General Hospital. Mrs. Weston was coming to tour the new maternal unit. A little knot of staff gathered round the side entrance, where she was scheduled to arrive at precisely 1:10 p.m.

The car pulled up. "Oh! Isn't she pretty!" sighed one woman happily. Her Honour alighted and immediately went to work. She greeted everyone in sight and moved gracefully ahead to inspect the newborns, trailed by a pack of cameras. She chatted up the new moms, cradled their infants, made gentle jokes with beaming dads in baseball caps and confided her own maternal experiences.

Most people would rather eat glass than do this for a living. It's hard work. By the end of 2001, Mrs. Weston had schlepped to Sudbury and Sarnia and Sioux Lookout. She had endured countless renditions of "O Canada" by fifth-graders. She had greeted Boy Scouts and lifesavers, Big Sisters and veterans. She had received dignitaries from Latvia, Romania, Madeira and obscure provinces in Mexico. She had approved 44,161 appointments of notaries and commissioners and signed 15,115 orders-in-council, to say nothing of endless birthday greetings to people turning ninety. She had been on duty every single New Year's Day.

Why? "It's not as if she had anything to prove," someone said once.

But she did. She had to prove that she was not just another billionaire's society wife.

"I've never been a lady who lunches," she told me. Not that there's anything wrong with that, she added hastily. "I've been very privileged . . . This is an opportunity to give back."

But being L-G was a way to shine in her own world, on her own terms. Before she got the job, she wrote some coffee-table books. She launched the garden show at the Royal Winter Fair. She did the usual good works, ran the family's houses, played with the international polo set (Prince Charles is on her husband's team) and went to Europe for the collections. But she always lived in the shadow of her husband.

Her diction is Princess Di–like: soft, upper class and British. She often refers to herself as "one." And she is as diligent in her duties as the Queen. "I have never cancelled an event for illness, sickness or anything like that!" she told me with pride. "It's unthinkable that I could cancel."

Like Princess Di, Mrs. Weston is good at the common touch. She cut down on protocol and got rid of the receiving lines. Wherever she went, she dropped in on the local women's shelter. She spent lots of time with people who will never get their names in the paper.

Mrs. Weston remembers what it was like not to be rich. She was the eldest of five children. Her father was an Irish appliance salesman who died when she was seventeen. She and her sisters went to work so that their brothers could go to college (that's what sisters were expected to do back then). Hilary Frayne's fresh blond beauty soon made her one of Ireland's top models. When she was twenty-one, Galen saw her picture on a billboard, and they got married three years later.

She's still a beauty today. She has age-appropriate bags and sags. Unlike almost every woman in her set, her face appears to be unrefreshed by the surgeon's knife. She doesn't like to wear much makeup. She is tall and toned and very slim and still looks spectacular in spaghetti straps. When her husband takes her onto the dance floor, they look completely happy.

Mrs. Weston has immaculate but conservative taste. That day at the hospital she was dressed in something charming, pink and expensive. On her feet were terrific two-tone sling-backs with stiletto heels. Unlike the more fashion-forward Madame Clarkson, she would never wear an outfit that made her look like Big Bird.

Following the baby tour, Mrs. Weston gave a short speech to the hospital staff and volunteers, listened to some Grade 5 students sing "O Canada," and presented an award she had initiated for volunteerism. The winner, an elderly lady named Helen Kubbinga, glowed with pride. The winner's family glowed. The audience glowed. You never would have guessed that she had done this about five thousand times before.

After she finished her term as L-G, Hilary Weston turned her talents to something even harder—raising money. Fundraising is a daunting task in Canada at the best of times, but these days it's a donor's market. In Toronto alone, six big arts institutions are competing for cash. As chair of Renaissance ROM, Mrs. Weston is leading the drive that will pay for Daniel Libeskind's transformation of the Royal Ontario Museum. Thanks to her, the ROM received a $30-million-dollar cheque from Michael Lee-Chin—the richest, most successful Canadian no one had ever heard of until then.

Mr. Lee-Chin and the ROM look like an unlikely match. He's a first-generation, self-made millionaire who arrived here from Jamaica when he was nineteen. For most of its history, the ROM has been a WASPy dowager from Rosedale.

The ROM needs Mr. Lee-Chin, and not just for his wallet. Venerable old institutions that depend on the shallow pool of Canada's old money—the Thomsons, the Westons, the Irvings, the Desmarais—are as doomed as the dinosaurs. The future is the two big M's: multiculturalism and meritocracy.

Daniel Libeskind's steel and glass entranceway to the ROM will carry Michael A. Lee-Chin's name. But the four-story atrium will be named for his mother, Hyacinth, who once had to use a box for his playpen. And the Westons will be nearby. They have naming rights for two new galleries. At a ceremony marking the museum's ninetieth birthday, Hilary announced that they'll be chipping in $20 million themselves.

How could I have been so snide? Mrs. Weston is the real thing. In spite of all her money, she has the type of class that money can't buy.

Who Needs the Windsors?

Because she reminds us we're not Americans, the Queen has become the last refuge of Canadian nationalists. "The monarchy is one of the few remaining threads in the Canadian identity," wrote artist Robert Bateman in a paean penned for the Queen's Golden Jubilee. "I sometimes think Americans are envious of our royal family. Unlike Disneyland, the monarchy is real with ancient roots and traditions."

Actually, many of the royal traditions are quite new. Toward the end of Victoria's reign, Britain's ruling elites began trumping up the role to disguise the fact that it was they who wielded the power. The monarch did not regularly open Parliament until well into the twentieth century. The investiture of the Prince of Wales was a ceremony resurrected in 1911.

The truth is that the monarchy stands for much that has held Canada back. It embodies the triumph of inheritance over merit, of blood over brains, of mindless ritual over innovation. The monarchy reminds us to defer to authority and remember our place. In Quebec, the royals are regarded as an insult.

It's a ghastly institution. And the Windsors aren't much better.

The best that can be said of the Queen is that she is diligent in her duties and has never done anything improper. One suspects she lacks the imagination for it. She likes her corgis better than her children (who, unlike the corgis, must make appointments when they want to see her). In fact, she doesn't care for people much at all.

Her children suffer from the curse of inherited wealth and boundless sycophancy, which are nearly always fatal to the development of character. For the most part dim and plain, they are living proof of the perils of inbreeding. Diana (who at least was able to connect with ordinary people) injected some attractive genes, but not smart ones. So her sons will generate a steady stream of entertaining scandal for the gutter press, the only institution that would truly suffer if the monarchy were done away with.

The Queen's husband is probably no more racist, sexist or snobbish than other men of his age and class. He is also reported to be charmless, boorish and rude. "I thought it was against the law these days for a woman to solicit," he once joked to a female solicitor. "It looks as though it was put together by an Indian," he said about a poorly wired fuse box he spotted on a factory tour. "If you stay here much longer, you'll get slitty eyes," he told a British student studying in China.

But the worst legacy of the monarchy to Canada is our parliamentary system, the one that we imagine makes us somehow superior to the Americans. Actually, it's the other way around. Our version of democracy has declined into a one-party state, where the ruling party is elected by a far smaller percentage of the voters but wields far more power than any group of politicians in the United States.

We like to deplore America's imperial presidents. But at least they are booted out from time to time. As for the House of Commons, for all its influence on the government and its contribution to the national debate, it might as well be filled with yapping corgis.

Walter Bagehot, the legendary British editor and thinker, believed that a prominent monarchy was necessary as a symbol of leadership to the ignorant working classes. He also wrote, "Among a cultivated population, a population capable of abstract ideas, it would not be required."

If we thought the monarchy still mattered, we'd have to have a revolution. Because we think it doesn't, we figure we might as well be gracious to the Queen when she visits. Polite to a fault, that's us. But the claim that she strengthens our national identity is pathetic. "The day will surely come," British journalist Joan Smith wrote, "when Buckingham Palace is turned into a theme park for foreign visitors who want to marvel at the revolting attitudes of the English upper classes."

As for the claim that the monarchy signifies our cultural superiority to you-know-who next door, forget it. Sorry, Mr. Bateman. Disneyland and the Windsors are both a form of spectacle, good only for amazing the tourist trade. Personally, I'll take Disneyland any day.

Chapter Ten

A Woman's Wisest Years

It takes me a long time to get out of the house these days. First I have to find my glasses, then my keys. Then I have to find my shoes. The other day I stopped to cash a cheque on the way to work. I locked the car and left the cheque in it, then got the cheque and locked the car again and left my pen in it. It took three tries to get it right, and then I left my umbrella in the bank.

Welcome to a woman's wisest years.

Yes, that's how they're billing it. Menopause is no longer a damn nuisance. It has been rebranded as a powerful tool for self-improvement.

"Menopause is an opportunity for unprecedented personal growth," promises Dr. Christiane Northrup, who is the reigning guru of the change of life. She herself is living proof. After she started having hot flashes, she dumped her husband, became a TV celebrity and wrote a book called *The Wisdom of Menopause,* which rode the best-seller lists for more than a year. Now she's rich and famous and has inner peace. Follow her advice, and this could happen to you.

Menopausal women are a terrific target market because there are so many of us. In the next decade, forty million women in North America will be going through the change. And since boomers always treat each stage of life as if they've personally invented it then amplify their revelations till everyone gets totally fed up, I know one thing for sure. Menopause is hot. Invest in yam-cream stocks.

In fact, it's so hot that even men are demanding a piece of the action. (How like them, I can hear you say.) Men are succumbing to a brand-new syndrome called andropause, which is similar to menopause because it makes you crabby and everything starts drooping. But men skip the New Age mumbo jumbo and go straight for the quick fix—a little testosterone gel.

Dr. Northrup says menopause rewires a woman's brain to make you more intuitive. She also says that your symptoms are not just physical in nature. Often they contain a message about your life.

"We are attracting precisely the illness or problem that best facilitates access to our inner wisdom," she explains. In her case, it was a fibroid (a benign uterine tumour). "I was trying to understand what my fibroid was trying to teach me," she writes. She discovered that the meaning of her fibroid was that her husband didn't understand her, and it was telling her to ditch him.

What is the hidden message of my forgetfulness? Why am I so crabby? What's the real reason the long-distance phone commercial on TV makes me weep uncontrollably? Maybe it means my mate and I are disconnected. Or maybe it means I forgot to pay the phone bill again.

The truth is, my symptoms haven't taught me much about my inner life. The only thing they've taught me is that I'd better paste yellow sticky notes on my computer whenever I'm supposed to meet someone for lunch. These days I phone up and leave messages for myself at work, then when I get to work I phone myself at home to do the same. Even so, I'm afraid I'm losing all my friends. "I really meant to phone you back," I'm explaining all the time, "but I'm going gaga."

The other day I blanked out on the words for "windshield scraper." English suddenly becomes a sort of foreign language, and you're forced to grope for synonyms for words that have gone AWOL. My friend Marcy is even worse than I am. Although she is able to talk brilliantly for hours about the field in which she is a leading authority, she can't remember the names of common household objects. "Where's that thing you use to mix the salad dressing?" she'll ask. "You know what I mean. That thing. With the wires." Frequently her sentences are completely unintelligible. "Can you lend me that fantastic novel by Saul Bellow, *The Bleeding Heart*?" she says, when what she means is *The Human Stain* by Philip Roth. She maintains that even though the things she says are factually inaccurate, they are generally true, which is what counts.

Marcy's theory is that we only have a certain number of memory slots in our brains, and by the time you reach age fifty they're all filled up. Your brain has no room for new information. This wouldn't be so bad if the information you already possessed was worth having. Unfortunately, my own memory slots are crammed with useless junk. I can scarcely recall a single thing I learned in five years of university. But I know the complete lyrics to every early Beatles tune, to say nothing of the *Howdy Doody* theme song.

It's nice to tell ourselves that aging is all about self-actualization. That way, maybe we'll forget that it's really about re-infantilization. The humiliating signs are everywhere. For example, I have finally given up and put my glasses on a string. It's a jaunty purple stretchy string, the kind that athletes wear. But it's still a string. And in my heart I know that I'll never be mistaken again for a surfer or a lifeguard.

"So I see you got the string," said a friend of mine the other day. "Just like mittens, huh?"

The other problem with conquering menopause (instead of just ignoring it and shutting up about it, the way my grandma did) is that it takes quite a bit of work.

It's not enough just to get in touch with your inner wisdom. You also have to eat vast amounts of soy products and ground flaxseed, become an expert on HRT (hormone replacement therapy), give up bread, cut down on booze, start lifting weights and do Pilates four times a week. You have to take your calcium supplements and antioxidants, practise biofeedback, get rid of all the negative people in your life and reconnect with your creative side. If you do all those things, plus have a facelift, perhaps you'll look and feel as good as Dr. Northrup. But even then you'll still need a string for your glasses.

We boomers are an optimistic lot. We're dedicated to the proposition that we can turn every bad thing that happens (divorce, fibroids, growing old, losing our short-term memory) into the next step in our personal spiritual transformation.

Twenty years from now Gail Sheehy will probably write a book about overcoming the challenge of personal mortality. It will be called *The Final Passage.* It will argue that death is a good thing. No doubt it will be a best-seller, too.

Beat the Clock

Give me that hair. Give me that voice. Give me that fabulous pair of legs. When I get old I want to be a red hot mama, just like Tina Turner strutting through a pantyhose ad. Never mind that Tina's hair isn't her own and that Tina's face and torso have no doubt been considerably enhanced by Photoshop. Tina has the right idea. She's decided to hold out as long as possible.

Tina is no anorexic teenager. She's getting on to seventy years old. If someone that old looks that good, maybe there's hope for the rest of us.

Is seventy the new forty? Could be. Consider the classic movie *Sunset Boulevard,* which featured a tragically faded star whose denial of aging turned her into a grotesque, pitiable monster. In the movie, Norma Desmond was fifty. When they turned *Sunset Boulevard* into a stage musical a few years ago, it starred a parade of fifty-something actresses who looked way too young for the part.

Vitamins, diet, exercise, hair dye and the knife are working miracles on us. They're also dramatically revising our ideas of what middle-aged women are supposed to look like. Today, ordinary women who look their age look increasingly odd. That's because we see more and more famous women who seem miraculously untouched by the ravages of time or menopause. Sophia Loren and Raquel Welch look exactly the way they did twenty years ago. Barbara Walters looks like a distant, younger, better-looking cousin of herself. When Joan Rivers and her daughter, Melissa, did their red-carpet thing at the Oscars, it was Melissa whose lines were showing.

Once upon a time, I swore I'd never be so vain as to submit to the knife. Once upon a time, I also knew for sure that I'd never get turkey neck. And then one day I woke up and there it was, a little wattle where my jawline used to be. So far as I'm concerned, nobody should be allowed to condemn cosmetic surgery until they're over fifty.

Today extreme-makeover shows are hits on prime-time TV. They let you have it both ways, deploring the pathetic losers who are so insecure they'll submit to radical surgery to improve their self-esteem while secretly thinking how much better you'd look if only you had your nose fixed.

Most of my friends are conflicted about the surgical road to eternal youth. We know it's a vain, unliberated form of self-improvement. But the entire culture tells us it's a sin to simply lapse into old age gracefully. You're supposed to fight it. The bookstores are crammed with first-person accounts from women gushing about how nifty it is to be fifty or sixty. In these books, the author invariably preaches tolerance and acceptance of the changes wrought by time, then goes on to relate how she herself overcame her middle-aged spread, sagging energy, cellulite and negative attitude with a dose of positive thinking and a new exercise regime. On the cover is a picture of the youthful-looking subject in a size-8 suit. Around page 122 she confesses that even though her butt is a bit saggy, her sex life has never been better, and the same can be true for you too.

These books all regard the body as an unruly wilderness to be tamed, cultivated, tended and groomed. They treat mental life the same way. It's hard to make fun of them, because they reflect our culture's underlying faith in progress and our belief in the virtues of hard work, self-improvement and self-control.

Ultimately, though, they're rather depressing. In the short run, they make it impossible for you to contemplate your flabby triceps without a twinge of self-reproach. You could do something about those if you really wanted to! And in the long run, you are faced with the certain knowledge that flabby triceps will one day be the least of your worries.

There are, of course, very good reasons for women to fear getting old. The stock of a post-menopausal woman in this culture sinks dramatically, and we all know it. Once upon a time there was a suitable role for women in late middle age as matriarchs, dowagers and queen bees—rulers of extended families, arbiters of social life, enforcers of community values. That role has disappeared, and my generation will all pass straight from the most extended youth in history to—what? The mind blanks out.

There's always the Germaine Greer option. You can simply give up the game, declare yourself to be an old crone and retire to your male-free zone in the English countryside to cultivate your peonies, write books and fantasize about the erotic power of adolescent boys. Few of us will be bold enough to follow her example, however. Most of us, like Tina Turner, would rather hold on to our attributes as long as humanly possible. She got lucky with those legs. They say the legs are the last to go.

Better You Than Me, Sister

Would you like to run a marathon? Lots of people would. It is the ultimate symbol of middle-aged self-actualization. My girlfriends are signing up in packs to join Jean's Marines, a gung-ho group that promises a transformational experience on the way to the finish line. Sure, your toenails will turn black and fall out. But that's part of the fun.

My invitation to join the Marines arrived in my e-mail on the dawn of the first day of a new year (no coincidence). "As you know by now, the only race that counts in life is the long run," it said.

I was hugely flattered. But I was also dubious. My personal history is a record of almost uninterrupted sloth; of lapsed health-club memberships, failed training regimens and barely used exercise equipment that hulks in a corner of the bedroom like a constant reproach.

Needless to say, my interior life is an endless feedback loop of guilt, self-recrimination and resolutions to try harder. Why can't I be like my friend Jane, whose sweaty running shoes I'm not fit to lick? Last year, she signed up for the marathon and finished it in 5:13. She is three years older than I am. She used to get up at five to train while I lolled around in bed. She ran up hills in thirty-degree heat all summer while I drank beer. She is good and I am bad. She never eats Cookie Dough Dynamo straight from the tub. She is going to heaven, and I am going to hell.

Yet as I sat in my PJs cataloguing my sins, it occurred to me (not for the first time) that healthism has become our new religion. How else can you explain a mass desire to run and run until you use up all your electrolytes and throw up? And yet the dogmas of healthism are unquestioned. We have all internalized them. Our leaders preach them from their pulpits and our media faithfully report their message. Instead of being photographed in church, politicians are now photographed practising good health habits to demonstrate their piety and civic virtue.

The churches may be deserted, but the gyms are full of the heaving, sweating faithful mortifying their flesh. Like all religions practised in cold northern climates, healthism requires plenty of strict self-denial. Some people even have a personal trainer, our age's version of a spiritual adviser.

For the most devout, there are special retreats, called spas. Nowadays, a spa is not a place that pampers you. Instead, it charges thousands of dollars a week to make you go on forced marches through the desert and survive on carrot juice. The less food you get, the more expensive it is.

In order to purify the flesh, not only must you starve, you must also purge. The latest in healthism is detoxification, which gets rid of the poisons that build up in your body from eating dangerous substances such as food. "Detoxifying treatments are on the rise," Mary Bemis, the editor of *American Spa*, told *The New York Times*. "I think people are becoming almost compulsive about ridding themselves of impurities."

Once it was a mark of status to show how much you could consume. Now it's a mark of status to show how much you can refrain from consuming. People who have cut out salt, sugar, fat, caffeine and alcohol are regarded as more virtuous and more moral than all the rest of us. Sloth, smoking, obesity and an addiction to Quarter Pounders are secretly regarded as lower class. Liberal egalitarians (who, of course, pretend that class does not exist) are certain that society would be far better off if only the lower orders gave up their sinful ways and learned to control their appetites.

These reflections give me a sharp craving for a Krispy Kreme. I do not, alas, adhere to Health Canada's food guidelines. I eat too much red meat and too few leafy greens. I have regularly failed to monitor my cholesterol or floss daily or schedule my yearly mammogram or stop after one glass of wine. I am a menace to public health and the sustainability of universal medicare.

But there is hope. Even the most hopeless couch potato can be turned into a marathoner in nine months. "Impossible as it may seem now, you'll be raising your arms in triumph as you cross the finish line," said my e-mail.

Yes! Yes! Yes! I thought. That could be me. But just as I was about to push the reply button and sign on, a new thought stayed my hand. Have we all gone crazy? What's so wrong with drinking beer? Whatever happened to the pleasure principle?

And how did the most hedonistic generation on earth turn into a bunch of self-righteous, guilt-ridden self-deniers?

I don't know the answers. But I do know that I zapped that e-mail into oblivion. And it felt good.

Chapter Eleven

I Married a Retrosexual

This is the story of how my husband got mugged in Shoppers Drug Mart.

It wasn't his fault, I suppose. On certain matters, he is as innocent as a newborn babe. Although he is a master of the infield-fly rule and can lucidly explain the neutral-zone trap, he should not be allowed to roam around unsupervised at cosmetics counters. In other words, he's a genuine guy.

Genuine guys are sometimes known as retrosexuals, to distinguish them from metrosexuals, who are men with the good taste of gay men, only they're straight. Metrosexuals are scrupulous about their grooming and are great consumers of men's cosmetic products. They use hair gel. Retrosexuals are scared of hair gel. Some people think that retrosexuals automatically have Neanderthal views about women, but this is not the case. A retrosexual is simply someone who doesn't know the difference between teal and aqua, and frankly couldn't give a damn.

Secretly, I've always thought that my husband could stand to be just a little bit more metro. Sometimes I buy him fancy shaving cream or scent with a designer name and leave it suggestively on his side of the sink. He never gets the hint. He prefers a ten-second dry shave, with a plastic disposable razor and toilet paper to staunch the wounds. If he's really in the mood he shaves with soap. He doesn't like anything too smelly.

From time to time, my husband's retrosexuality bothers me. For example, he can't understand why it's time to paint the kitchen when we just painted it nine years ago. He doesn't get why we need expensive matchstick blinds on all the kitchen windows, which we leave permanently rolled up. He's baffled that my haircuts cost ten times more than his do, and he thinks massages are a waste of time, except for one he got from two masseuses on the beach at Phuket.

But there are certain advantages to my husband's retrosexual orientation, and they are large. For example, being completely indifferent to appearance, a retrosexual will never complain that you're putting on weight. This is one of the foundation stones of a good marriage. Also, it's easy to impress him with your culinary prowess. My husband is so grateful to get out of kitchen duty that he brags about my cooking, even though it's usually quite lousy. In return, he allows me to weasel out of certain household tasks like garbage duty and disposing of the mice the cat brings home.

He knows it's his job to talk to plumbers and electricians, man to man. We are aware that we have lapsed into tired gender stereotypes. We don't care. We only wish there were a third gender to clean the kitty litter. We have resolved our primal conflicts over housework by employing a Portuguese cleaning lady once a week and drastically lowering our (okay, my) standards on the other six days. This is another foundation stone of a good marriage.

In a way, I blame myself for the mugging in the Shoppers Drug Mart. I never should have let him go alone. Something similar would have happened to me if I'd wandered into Future Shop all by myself and tried to buy a fancy new TV. The chance of a good outcome was remote.

The trouble began when he noticed that his shins were dry and itchy. (He blames his new ski socks.) So he went off to Shoppers to get something to rub on them. Instead of heading for the aisle filled with Jergens, Keri Lotion and Vaseline, he stopped at the cosmetics counter and asked the cute girl there for her advice. "Moisturizer," he said. "I need moisturizer. I don't want anything smelly. I don't want to smell like a girl."

He was quite excited when he got home. "This will do the trick," he said. "It's got lipidins in it." I asked him what lipidins were, and he said the cosmetics consultant told him they lock in your natural moisture. He proudly showed me a small plastic bottle filled with something called Vichy Re-Lipidising Body Cream-Fluid. It came in a special aqua-coloured tote bag. According to the label, the ingredients included genuine Vichy thermal-spa water from France, which probably explains why the bottle cost forty-three dollars.

"You've been mugged," I said.

"I thought it was a bit expensive," he confessed. He was too intimidated to complain about the price. He didn't know that he could have got some Vaseline Intensive Care (no Vichy water, no lipidins) for $3.99.

Naturally, I've teased him mercilessly ever since. But the truth is, I really have no interest in men who are interested in skin care. That can be my job. In return, I'm happy to let them worry about the oil level in the car. Some might call this sexist. I call it a sensible division of labour, and it is one of the chief benefits of marriage. Each of you can specialize. And each of you can sometimes get away with acting like a helpless bunny.

Not surprisingly, my husband was too embarrassed to take back his re-lipidising cream, and today he's probably the only male in the world who's rubbing it on his itchy shins. "I'm locking in my moisture," he says defiantly.

I don't have the heart to tell him it makes him smell like a girl.

Treat Him Like a Gerbil

For years, Dr. Laura was one of my guilty pleasures. I'd dial her up on the radio and listen in fascinated horror as she flayed her callers for their moral cowardice. "Dump him!" she'd screech at some hapless single mother whose new boyfriend didn't get along with the kids. "So quit!" she'd order some poor woman whose husband complained that she was spending too much time at her job. "What are you waiting for?"

In Laura Schlessinger's moral world there are no compromises. Divorce is bad. Cheating on your spouse is worse. She doesn't feel your pain—she's there to dish it out. I often wonder why people bother calling her. Are they masochists? Or do they secretly hope she will stiffen their spines for them?

Dr. Laura's radio career is in decline, but her publishing career is more robust than ever. Her latest book, *The Proper Care & Feeding of Husbands,* hit Number One in Edmonton and Omaha. Her central message is really very simple: if you want to improve your marriage, be nicer to your husband. Give him a hug when he comes home from work. Cook him dinner and sit down to eat it with him. Stop nagging. Have sex with him whenever he wants.

Yes, really.

But wait. Is this not a two-way street?

Nope. It's up to you, honey. According to Dr. Laura, it's women, not men, who are primarily in control of the relationship. Tend to his needs, and he'll be so grateful he'll tend to yours. "Men are simple creatures, really," she says. They're not all that much more complicated than gerbils. Give them food and affection, and they'll be eating out of your hand in no time.

Not surprisingly, Dr. Laura heaps a pile of scorn on the feminist project. Feminism, she says, has not only taught women to criticize men for not meeting their needs, but has also taught women to ignore the needs of men. Feminism has replaced old-fashioned notions of duty and responsibility with the idea that a woman's first duty is to fulfill herself.

It's not hard to dump on Dr. Laura. Her psychology of the sexes is ridiculously simplistic. She doesn't practise what she preaches (she's been divorced, she's posed in the nude, and in her house her husband does the cooking). She is a first-class harridan. She also has more serious problems, starting with her flat-out rejection of homosexuality. So it pains me to admit that she's on to something.

A lot of women I know have a sort of balance-sheet approach to a relationship. (I am not entirely innocent in this regard.) This mentality has been fuelled by the grievance culture of feminism. For the past thirty years, women have been chronicling all the ways that men fail to pull their weight and how unfair it all is. So he forgot to take out the garbage again? That's another debit. The poor schnook is always overdrawn at the marital bank, and he doesn't even know it. He has no idea how busy we are—out earning money, making the grocery list, schlepping the kids around and remembering his mother's birthday—and he doesn't have a clue how exhausted all that makes us. And then, he wants to have sex! The nerve. Doesn't he realize we're too tired and mad at him?

Here's Dr. Laura's advice. Get over it. And by the way, shave your legs and lose the sweatpants.

The idea that a woman has obligations to her husband, especially sexual ones, is deeply disconcerting. It sounds primitive and submissive. Since when are wives supposed to serve up sex on demand?

And yet Dr. Laura's got a point. It's not totally untrue to say that sex is to men what intimate conversation is to women—a way of emotionally connecting with the person you care most about. It's his way of asking you to pay attention to him.

Some of the best marriages I know involve couples who just missed the feminist wave. These men and women are in their sixties now. I used to pity the wives, who sacrificed their identity (read: career) in order to stay home and manage Family Inc. I used to think these women must be bitter, narrow and resentful. Then I got to know some of them. I was astonished to discover that they're smart, engaged and contented, and that their husbands adore them. No one could doubt that these marriages are made of equal partners.

This type of marriage is deeply out of fashion. Women who stay at home have zero social status, as feminists have correctly noted. But feminism has made it worse, by caricaturing them as Stepford wives.

The most radical thing Dr. Laura has to say is that it's not all about you after all. You come third, after your spouse and kids, in that order. Forget your grievances and entitlements. If he's not asking for sex, make him a ham sandwich and dig out the old negligee. If you do right by him, she promises that he'll swim through shark-infested waters to bring you lemonade. Treat him like a gerbil, and he'll treat you like a queen.

Six Degrees of Separation

To the outside world, my husband and I are the most compatible of couples. But what does the outside world know? The truth is we suffer from a form of marital dysfunction that no amount of therapy can fix, not even Dr. Laura's.

He likes it hot, and I like it cold.

To be precise, he likes to set the thermostat at seventy-five. My ideal is sixty-nine. (If you want this in Celsius, you'll just have to look it up.) These six degrees of separation are our family curse. They are responsible for nearly twenty years of low-level skirmishing and minor sniping, of simmering resentment (mine) and cool disdain (his).

In matters involving money, politics and even in-laws, we live in happy harmony. But when it comes to climate control, we're cats and dogs together. He detests air conditioning; I can't survive without it.

I've never met a couple who are thermostatically compatible. But my husband and I were indeed unlucky to find each other. "With most couples, it's the man who gets too hot," says Marsha Ackermann, the world's leading (and perhaps only) cultural historian of air conditioning. "Women can tolerate heat about two degrees Fahrenheit better than men do. So you're very unusual."

We owe our woes to Willis Carrier, who installed the first air conditioner a century ago. The father of the air conditioner did not set out to rescue sweltering humanity. He was trying to solve a production problem for a printing press that couldn't get the ink to adhere to glossy paper when the weather was hot and humid. Mr. Carrier invented a device that could control both temperature and humidity in the printing process.

For many years, air conditioning was used only to enhance industrial productivity. Then, in 1924, a Detroit department store installed it in the bargain basement, so that customers could shop all summer long. Movie theatres installed it to attract business, and it became an instant hit. Then businesses began putting it in office buildings so that workers would become more productive, too. Today, we can work and shop every day all summer long, with no time off for naps. This is widely considered to be progress.

My husband and I have little hope of resolving our differences. His idea of a nice place to visit is Bangkok. He likes strolling through the outdoor markets at midday and eating at the noodle stands as the all-day traffic gridlock emits noxious fumes. My view is, why go all the way to Bangkok when you can just stand inside a blast furnace and suck on an exhaust pipe?

When we travel, he actually prefers to stay in places without air conditioning. He claims the noise keeps him awake and the air gives him a cold. When I complain about the heat, he wraps himself in blankets and starts to sniffle.

When I moved into his house, there was a king-sized Jacuzzi but no air conditioning. He openly suspects that my suffering in the summer heat is a sign of weak character. Only when we got engaged did he relent. I told him I wouldn't marry him unless he did.

Now we have a little house in the country. It's on a hill, so he convinced me that the breeze would keep it nice and cool. It would—if only we lived in Banff. But in Ontario, the saturated, stifling summer air spares no one.

"Please, please, please, can we get air conditioning?" I whine, lying supine and dripping on the couch. In the car, at least, we have a deal. The driver gets to control the temperature, and the other one has to maintain silence for as long as possible.

According to Ms. Ackermann, my husband is not a nut. His aversion to air conditioning was once shared by the patrician class, which had other ways to fight the heat—breezy summer houses by the sea, servants to sweat for them. FDR had Washington air-conditioned to improve the efficiency of the bureaucracy but refused to have air conditioning in the

White House. To bohemians and other critics of the bourgeoisie, it was a symbol of the bland conformity of American life. (Henry Miller wrote a book called *Air-Conditioned Nightmare.*)

Air conditioning is one of those cultural transformers, like electricity. It's brought year-round comfort to the masses. Without it, there would be no high-rise office buildings, no indoor shopping malls, no New South. There would also be no computers, or any of the vast scientific research that relies on precise temperature and humidity calibration.

As for marital incompatibility, Ms. Ackermann has problems, too. She likes it hot, her husband not. "We keep it at seventy-eight during the day and then turn it down at night," she says. "He likes it cooler, but he also likes to save money."

I am married to a frugal Scot with mixed patrician and bohemian blood. Meantime, I think I'm having hot flashes. Can this marriage be saved? Maybe—when September rolls around.

Our Reclining Years

Several Christmases ago, my husband and I decided to buy ourselves a treadmill. It was one of those *folies à deux* that married people fall into. We would start to work out at last. We would get into shape, right in our own home! Of course we could always go outside and walk, but it's cold outside. You can't watch CNN. Convenience, we rationalized, would ensure our road to fitness.

You know what happened. We set the thing up in our bedroom and used it a few times. Then we stopped. There it sat, a constant reproach to our sloth. Sometimes I would dry my underwear on it. Eventually I got my husband to move it downstairs to an obscure corner just outside his office. It was big and ugly, but pretty soon we didn't notice it anymore, except when people came over for dinner and asked, "What's that?"

Every year or two, I would suggest that we get rid of it, or at least move it to the basement. My husband always said no. Any time now he might want to get back on it.

Many men are this way, I've found. They are inherently conservative (or perhaps simply delusional). They don't believe in getting rid of anything, because some time it might be useful again. Or maybe they're just nostalgic. Who knows? Maybe that brown corduroy chair mouldering in the basement reminds them of their youth, when they thought people who owned treadmills were ridiculous.

Like everyone else, my husband and I worry a lot about the statements our possessions make about us. "Is there anything more bourgeois than this?" we asked the day we went out shopping for expensive patio furniture. We decided that there was not. We were sad about that. There is, however, something more bourgeois than patio furniture: it is a reclining chair.

I don't remember who first broached the subject of a reclining chair. Whoever it was, was subjected to a torrent of abuse. Because reclining chairs mean just one thing: Homer Simpson.

"Over my dead body," I said. Or maybe it was him.

But we had a big corner in the living room where a person could stretch out and a comfy chair would be ideal. And gradually we came to agree that a reclining chair might be all right, providing it didn't look like one.

Finding a reclining chair that lacks the Homer Simpson factor is not as easy as you think. There seemed to be no other kind. We saw recliners covered in brown corduroy, recliners with levers on the side and recliners with cup holders in the arms like movie seats. We saw his'n'hers recliners that came with TV-dinner trays in the middle, and electric recliners that plugged in. All were hideous. One night, we drove to the farthest reaches of Mississauga to visit the biggest La-Z-Boy store in Ontario. I was terrified that we might run into somebody we knew, though of course there was no chance of that.

At last, after around a year of looking, we found a decent-looking chair in a store just around the corner, and bought it instantly.

Now we fight each other for reclining time. Our friends come to mock, but stay to lounge. "You got what?" screeched a girlfriend of mine, a person of impeccable taste. Then she came over and plopped herself in it, put her feet up and refused to get out.

Now that we have entered our reclining years, I figured I might finally be able to persuade my husband to part with the treadmill. It was during one of those periods when you look around your house and discover it's a dump, so you run around throwing out your useless junk and painting the kitchen. "Okay," he groused, "so long as I don't have to think about it."

I figured I should seize the moment before he changed his mind. So I phoned up the fitness emporium that had sold it to us. I reasoned that they would be well acquainted with the market for second-hand, barely used exercise equipment. They told me to call somebody named Mike, who quoted me twenty cents on the dollar. I said fine. He came round to inspect it. It was covered with a thick film of greasy dust, and when they turned it on, it squealed. He quickly reduced his offer to $150. I said fine. He wrote me a cheque and took it away. Little did he know that I gladly would have paid him.

Proud of my efficiency, I waited for my husband to notice that the eyesore that had stood gathering dust for the past five years was gone. He didn't. A week went by, then two. "Don't you notice something different around here?" I asked one day. "Sure," he said. "We got the kitchen painted."

I've been thinking about how to spend the hundred and fifty bucks. Perhaps I'll buy a nice bottle of champagne and some genuine foie gras. Then I'll find a good book and settle back in our new recliner for an extremely pleasant evening. Maybe I'll give him some of the champagne. Or maybe not.

Too Stupid for Our Stuff

A few weeks ago, my husband and I finally succumbed and got a dish. Our excuse was our desire to liberate ourselves from the clutches of the evil cable company. Now we're free—sort of. My husband can watch *Law & Order* twenty-four hours a day, but I can't turn the TV on.

The truth is that I'm too stupid to operate the stuff I own. Our living room is littered with three or four remotes. One of them turns on the satellite, and one turns on the TV, and another turns on the DVD player, which we had to buy because our VCR is obsolete. I don't know what the other one does.

"You need a universal remote!" someone told me the other day. Meantime, I have to find my spouse whenever I want to watch the news. Then I have to find the news. I think it's on Channel 371. But who can remember?

This is the paradox of progress. The digital improvement of every product used in daily life has rendered us increasingly incompetent. We don't understand how to use the things we own. We used to be worried about our growing alienation from the natural world. Now, we're alienated from our refrigerators.

I have a car clock that's still on standard time. I don't know how to change it. The owner's manual no doubt tells me how, but by the time I find the manual we'll probably be on standard time again.

There are six or seven digital clocks in our house, all of them dysfunctional. Every time the power fails, they all start blinking 00:00. The clock-radio alarm on our night table is so sophisticated, you have to be a genius to set it. We aren't. Whenever we try, it goes off randomly in the middle of the night. So we don't use it anymore.

I can barely use our phone, although I have mastered "redial." At least it's simpler than my husband's cellphone, which has so many different features that it makes my head hurt. Then there's our brand-new digital camera, which can take pictures in any shape and size and store up 260 of them at a time. If only we could remember how to download them.

Back in the analogue days, you didn't have to take a course to turn on your TV, make a phone call or snap a photo. Any idiot could do it. Then came microchips. Now everything has fifteen gigabytes, and new products compete on the basis of how many features are crammed into them. That's why you can now buy a refrigerator that surfs the Internet.

But it's my computer that gives me the most exquisite feeling of incompetence. I've always approached my computer on a strictly need-to-know basis, but I've never known quite enough. Things disappear into my C drive, whatever that is, never to be seen again. I have two thousand ancient e-mails carefully sorted into folders I don't know how to delete. I can't create files or do attachments. I can't even kill off that stupid dancing paper clip. I'm ashamed at my ignorance, but asking for help after all this time would be too humiliating.

I found that I am not alone. I had to take a remedial Word course and discovered with relief that many of my highly trained, intelligent colleagues don't know how to cut and paste either.

The problem with computers is that they can do too much. They are ridiculously overengineered. I still don't have a clue what my C drive is, but I can now print my stories in any typeface upside down or sideways. I can even make them glitter. If I really want to make a point, I can access more than six dozen different types of wingdings.

"What's a wingding?" asked my husband, who regards my fear of electronics as a form of learned helplessness. I said I'd show him my wingdings if he forgives me for dropping the TV the day he wired the satellite receiver to it. I was bracing the TV with my knee while he crawled behind it, but it slipped and crashed on the floor. It wasn't really my fault. When we picked it up, Jack McCoy had turned green.

Behind our TV is the snake's nest of wires and cables that everybody has these days. It's a fact that all cultures have a primal fear of snakes, which explains why I don't want anything to do with them. A main reason I got married was to have someone else to do it. Hooking up electronic stuff is something all men like to think they are proficient at, like getting somewhere without ever asking for directions.

But now the guys are becoming alienated, too. My husband may not want to admit it, but hooking up a stereo has gone the way of car repair—a job once accessible to amateurs and now best left to experts. Even they don't always get it right. Some friends of mine got the best professionals to install their new plasma, hi-D, split-screen TV. The first time they turned it on, they got the face of Peter Mansbridge with the voice of Homer Simpson.

Sadly, getting rid of the snake's nest behind our TV will require a paid consultant. We already have one for our home computers. A nerd who makes house calls is now a middle-class necessity.

Now that we've got the satellite hooked up, I can report that having five hundred channels at your fingertips is kind of like having six dozen wingdings. All that choice is nice, but somewhat pointless. About four hundred and fifty channels carry programs that are fairly far down on my must-see list, like NASCAR races. And you can't get choice without complexity. Now I have to consult two different TV guides, one to figure out what's on and one to figure out where. By the time I find my reading glasses, go through the TV guides and get my husband to turn on the set for me, whatever it was I wanted to watch is nearly over.

So mostly we watch *Law & Order*. Fortunately, the green tint eventually went away.

As for the clock problem, I found the ideal solution at Pottery Barn. It's wireless. It has hands. It even ticks, although I think the tick is fake. It has no functionality at all. No radio, no CD player, no snooze-alarm. All it does is tell the time and wake you up. To change the time, you twist a little knob. To set the alarm, you point a little pointer at the time you want to wake up, then pull up a big knob on top. When the alarm goes off, you push it down.

That's all it does. That's it. It's perfect.

Chapter Twelve

Women without Men

When men and women need to get away from each other, they head off in vastly different directions. Men play poker; women go shopping. When men need a longer break, they retreat to the wilderness together. The classic male buddy experience is the fishing trip, where men can belch and not shave, and eat pan-fried steak and drink beer, pee outside and kill small animals. This is their idea of a really good time.

Where, then, do women go for a really good time? They go to the spa. Men, do not snicker. A week at the spa is much harder work than a week at the lake. And a week at the spa in the company of one hundred and forty other women revealed more to me about contemporary gender differences than all the feminist treatises in North America strung end to end.

Perhaps you think that spas are full of idle, bored, rich wives who like to be pampered with pedicures and cosseted in herbal wraps. Not so. The spa of today is full of driven, stressed-out career women who work too hard and pay their own bills. They tackle their spa week like any other major project, only this time the project is themselves.

A well-spent day at the spa begins with reveille at 5:30 a.m. and a brisk hike before breakfast up and down a mountain. Maybe eight kilometres or so. It continues with classes to tone, firm, stretch and tighten or loosen every conceivable body part. The schedule is crammed with Pilates, Fitball, Feldenkreis, Aquabics and Dynabands. It is all very scientific, and strenuous.

In case you're caught with an idle moment, there are lectures on menopause and astronomy to improve your mind. There are courses in meditation to improve your soul. And instead of killing small animals to demonstrate your skill, you can go to crafts class and make a wreath out of native plants and flowers. (That's the difference between hunters and gatherers, I guess.)

Needless to say, there's not a pan-fried steak in sight. Instead you eat legumes prepared in more ways than you dreamed were possible, and drink gallons of good honest water. All the women marvel at the creativity of the chef. All the men (there will be no more than five, all towed along by their wives) complain bitterly about the food and plot to sneak off to town for margaritas and a big juicy piece of meat.

It is a mistake to believe that these women's drive for self-improvement is rooted in vanity and narcissism. Just the opposite is true. It is rooted in guilt and self-criticism. Women, unlike men, are sure they are not okay. They are intimately acquainted with their flaws of both body and character, and they know whose fault it is: theirs. The woman who expires halfway up the mountain says things like, "Gee, I've really let myself go lately." The man who falters says things like, "Well, I sprained my ankle so I couldn't get to the gym for the last three months."

But the most distinguishing feature of women in groups is the ambient chat. Women communicate ceaselessly. One day I hiked for eleven kilometres up and down the mountain with four people, formerly total strangers, who never stopped talking even on the uphills. I don't remember a word anyone said. But by the end of it we were all great friends.

We chatted on the mountains, over our legumes, in the pool. We considerately made sure everyone got their proper share of air time. We kept chatting all week until we were wrenched apart at the airport, after many hugs and kisses and sincere vows to send photos, keep in touch, meet again next year. None of those things will happen, but that's not the point. The point is that all this chat made everyone feel connected.

Men use chat to extract information and establish status. They think small talk is inconsequential, and of course they're wrong. A great deal of small talk is really about values—who behaved well, who behaved badly and why. And all small talk is about relating. The medium is the message, remember?

As I flew back to frigid Toronto, full of vegetables and bursting with endorphins, I read a fascinating article about bonobos, a little-known but extremely amiable species of primate where the females, not the males, are in charge. The bonobos' social structure is maintained by friendly alliances between mature females, who stick up for each other if the males get out of line. No chest-thumping, teeth-baring chimp behaviour here. The females won't put up with it. Bonobos are peaceable, egalitarian and sociable. Of course they can't talk, so instead of constant friendly chat they have constant friendly sex—hetero, homo, intergenerational, you name it—to show they like each other. Another amiable feature of bonobo females is that they do not care about self-improvement.

The bonobos are hot right now because they offer sociobiologists a rare glimpse of a society that is not ruled by alpha males. To find out more about what such a society is like, you can go to the jungles of Zaire. Or you can join a few dozen women at a spa. It's not a bad way to spend a week.

A Passion for Stilettos

Spikes are hot. Spikes are big. And spikes are everywhere. Carrie and her *Sex and the City* pals may have tottered off the air for good, but if you don't have three or four good pairs of stilettos to cripple your feet, you're still a fashion nobody.

Spikes are evidently suitable for every season. Last November I spotted some stiletto heels on the boots of a model strutting across the cover of a glossy fashion brochure. With them, she was wearing a kicky little miniskirt—just the ensemble for your typical Canadian winter.

I spotted more spikes on page 734 of *Vogue*, which featured a Ralph Lauren boot with a chrome spike heel and black crocodile skin leather, available to you for $9,500 (U.S.). "After several seasons of sensible shoes, it's high time designers upped the danger quotient with pointed toes, ice-pick heels and a heady dose of attitude," went the editor's blurb.

Spikes are front and centre at Holt Renfrew, where they are mounted on a pedestal with what looks like museum lighting. What you want are evening sandals with maximum foot exposure and only a few artfully entwined straps of fabric to keep them from falling off your feet. They have a little silver buckle at the side, and stiletto heels that are four inches high. They cost $525 plus GST and PST. I badly wanted them. Alas, the extremely tall, elegant and forbidding man in the shoe department informed me crisply that most sizes were already sold out. It was obvious that he didn't think I was qualified to stroke the merchandise.

A stiletto heel only looks right on a shoe with a sharp pointy toe. Either end would make an effective weapon. The combination creates footwear that is completely impractical and requires the wearer to put up with a considerable amount of discomfort. "Naturally you'll have to practise walking in them," said the saleswoman who sold my friend Linda a pair of Manolos for a rock-bottom $445. But of course Linda will look fabulously spectacular in them. She's blonde and six feet tall, and her Manolos will make her six foot four.

According to the British Physics Institute, a 100-pound woman in stilettos will exert pressure under her foot that is twenty times that of a 6,000-pound elephant.

That's why they're so hard to walk in. But if you amputate your little toe, it helps. It also helps if the wearer is not actually required to walk at all. "How do people get around in these things?" I asked one sales associate. "You don't walk in them," she explained. "You pose."

Stilettos make a lot of statements about a woman. One statement they make is, "I take cabs everywhere." But you still have to get from the cab to the front door. City sidewalks are booby-trapped with grates, manholes and other shoe-mines that will shred the precious fabric on those heels faster than you can say Jimmy Choo. You can't drive with them on either. Nor are they suitable for wearing outdoors at any time from November to April, when salt, snow and slush will wreck them in two minutes (providing you don't slip and break your neck first).

The reigning king of stilettos is Manolo Blahnik. He is so famous that people who own his shoes refer to them simply as Manolos. He describes what he does as theatre for the feet. He recently did a shoe with long thin straps that tied all the way up the leg to the knee, decorated with satin leaves and rosebuds. It takes half an hour to put on, and it sold like crazy.

The classic Manolo is a slinky pump that is cut very low on the sides and through the toes to get maximum foot nudity. These scraps of leather are all attached to a towering stiletto. Sometimes there are ribbons and sometimes there are ostrich feathers. Mr. Blahnik is known as an engineering genius because it's possible to stand up in his shoes without falling off.

"I know how to cut away and still get a shoe to stay on the foot," he says. "I know how to make a heel eleven centimetres high and still balance properly. I know the secret of toe cleavage." It will not surprise you to learn that Mr. Blahnik is a favourite of foot fetishists, who have built temples to him on their Web sites.

I am not a foot fetishist. I am a sober, sensible Canadian, who faithfully contributes to her RRSP, dresses warmly in winter and is proud not to be a fashion victim. (So I once spent my entire allowance on a pair of white go-go boots. Didn't everyone?) I am prudent and thrifty. My social calendar is not filled with opening-night galas, and my favourite footwear is a nice warm pair of booties filled with duck down.

Why, then, did those stilettos in Holt's pierce me to the heart with a longing so great that I would happily have handed over a month's mortgage money to possess them?

You might as well ask why a guy goes out and spends $68,000 for a Porsche that he mainly drives to work and that won't hold two bags of groceries and that sprains your back when you try getting out of it. The Porsche is useless in the winter too.

But he loves it, because that machine gives him a sense of mastery. In it, he feels less Canadian, and quite a bit more interesting. Perhaps other people might imagine that he is a purring love machine.

It's the same with stilettos. Plus, they make you look five pounds lighter. Let the tumbrels roll. I've got to get some.

What Is Sex? A Dominatrix Demands

Terri-Jean Bedford, the resplendent mistress of fantasy, is showing me a pair of size-14 patent-leather high heels. "We get everything in extra large, because most of our clients are six feet tall," she says. She shows me some extra-large wedding dresses and a lacy white nightie with gauze wings, suitable for a cross-dressing fairy princess. She's got corsets in tight, extra tight and unbelievably tight; French maid costumes, wigs and eyeshadow. "These big fat hairy bald men need to feel attractive," she explains. On the wall are photos of a happy client in a maid costume, being spanked. In real life, he's a baker.

Terri-Jean—entrepreneur, civil libertarian and proprietor of a new venture called the Millicent Farnsworth Sissy Maid Academy & Charm School—is best known as the Bondage Bungalow Dominatrix. Back in the nineties she was busted for running an S&M operation in a sleepy Toronto suburb. The sting required a lengthy investigation and no fewer than fifteen cops, who dressed up in wigs, brandished whips and pretended to lick the boots of her employees to gather incriminating evidence.

A judge found her guilty of keeping a bawdy house but neglected to say whether whipping, bondage and humiliation are actually illegal. Terri-Jean argues they're not. The essence of prostitution is genital contact, and genital contact is not what she does. So she went to the Ontario Court of Appeal seeking to get her conviction overturned. She wants the appeal court judges to decide once and for all what is illegal sex and what is legal entertainment so that she can carry on her business as a dominatrix in peace.

Terri-Jean Bedford has a bountiful imagination, a keen sense of parody, good performance skills and an encyclopedic knowledge of paraphilia. She's a lot of fun to pass the time with. She told me that paraphiliacs, who are mostly men, can be aroused only by behaviour that is quite specific, atypical and extreme. Some of it is disgusting, and some is downright amazing.

"Psychotentiginous," she explains. "That describes people who are only aroused by cold weather." I ask if she's ever met a psychotentigiac. "No," she says, "but I do know people who like to be immersed in cold baths." Or dressed up like babies. "I act as a paratherapist," she says. "I offer fantasy recreation."

Before showing me around her dungeon, Terri-Jean read me part of a poem she'd written:

> *She's a just crusader, fighting for the right*
> *To discipline the bottoms of men both day and night.*

"I spank," she says, "but what about tattoos? Tattoos are legal! And they're permanent!"

Sadly, the S&M dungeon business isn't all that good these days. The clients have been scared off by her notoriety, and several other dominatrixes have set up competing dungeons around town. So Terri-Jean has worked hard to develop the Sissy Maid Academy, which is conducted upstairs in a genteel mock-Victorian parlour and seems to operate within the law. "Learn to Walk, Talk & Act Like A Lady!" reads the Sissy Maid brochure, which is printed in ladylike script. A private lesson costs $150 an hour (parking included). You can choose from classes entitled Girl Talk, Essentials of Submissiveness, Ladies' Maid Training and Petticoat Discipline. You can even go to Sissy Girl Camp Getaway for an entire weekend ($1,200 plus GST), which includes a Victorian dress-up tea party in the backyard next door. There are a lot of rules. If you break them, you might get spanked. Or you might have to write "I will finish my homework on time" a hundred times in longhand. People actually pay for this.

"And here is Madame's Petite Dungeon," says Terri-Jean as she leads me downstairs. We inspect the stocks, the bed of nails, the restraining devices, the cages (both full-body and head-only), the spanking bench and the blindfolds, feathers and whips. There's also a big Bible and a confessional, for penitents. I guess you could call it kinky, but, frankly, it seems about as sinister as a props-rental shop. The scariest item is the red-satin-lined coffin, in which she shuts people up.

"Sometimes I climb into it myself," she says. "It's very restorative. Sensory deprivation is a wonderful tool for problem-solving."

Terri-Jean keeps all her trial transcripts in a box under the lace-covered Victorian tea table in the parlour. She has a formidable legal team. It includes a prominent law professor, Alan Young, who's been working on her case for free. "I specialize in the area of consensual crime," he told me. "Unless there's a compelling reason to interfere, what people do in private should be their own private choice."

Mr. Young confesses he doesn't understand how grown men can get a kick out of dressing up in frilly panties and abasing themselves. "But I have trouble understanding stamp collectors, too." Besides, he adds, "it's the most fun I've ever had in court."

The French Do It Better

Nice girls don't. If they must, it is only because they have to, and they are not supposed to enjoy it. If they do, they keep it secret, even from their closest friends. Do it in public? People will be disgusted.

But we all know that sometimes, nice girls do. In a moment of weakness they simply lose control. Even the most resolute among us are not always immune to the pleasures of the flesh, even though we know the price we'll pay for those few moments of ecstasy is terrible indeed. We will drink the bitter draught of remorse, guilt and self-reproach. We will atone. We will mortify the flesh and resolve to be a better and more virtuous person—until the next time.

I am talking, of course, about eating: not the sort of minced, pinched, portion-controlled, disciplined, Protestant low-fat, low-cholesterol, low-everything eating that is the only acceptable form of eating today for middle-class North American women, but real eating, with creamy oozing cheeses, crackly buttery croissants with chocolate inside, juicy duck with crunchy fried duck fat and plump moist omelettes crammed with truffles, all washed down with enough Bergerac and Monbazillac and Armagnac to horrify every expert who nags us that for healthy, happy hearts and livers we ought never, ever to exceed six drinks a week.

It is, mercifully, not possible to fully indulge these pleasures of the flesh in Canada, where they are mostly unavailable, sometimes illegal and universally frowned upon. One must go to decadent France, the world's most sumptuous food bordello. In France, half the population is engaged in growing, procuring, selling and lovingly preparing food for the other half, which devotes a serious amount of time and thought to eating it.

France is a nation where dinner theatre is exactly that: a three-hour performance with at least three acts, but preferably five or six, all designed to ravish the audience and send them away at the end moaning with pleasure. Among the greatest delights of dining in France are all the treats that arrive unordered: *amuse-bouches* and *amuse-geules* and sorbets and plates of little sweets and wafers, and then some nougat and candied fruit to stuff in your pocket and take home. A serious French kitchen, like a great lover, is devoted to generosity and surprise.

The French believe that North Americans are prudish adolescents with coarse tastes (although they do have a soft spot for Canada on account of Iraq). They are the opposite of us because they do not take sex seriously, but they do take food seriously. In other words, they are a mature civilization.

In North America, you have to go out of your way to get really good food. In France, really good food is all around you. The Saturday morning market in the smallest country town is the scene of a thousand small seductions. Here is the weathered old cheese farmer, beckoning with tasty morsels of the finest *fromage de brebis*. There is the goat lady, with her pungent little rounds of *cabécou*, made from goats she milked herself. (There is not one kind of goat cheese. There are hundreds.) The truffle lady explains, in detail, the difference between black and white truffles and between winter and summer truffles, and the proper use of each. We get to sniff. The mushroom lady flaunts her furled *pleurottes* the size of your hand. They are pink and feel like baby flesh.

We are so weak with desire that we must rush to the café in the square and order several large cups of *café crème* with giant slabs of *tarte aux noix*. The café is jammed. At the next table, some farmers in berets and their wives are visiting and downing a few bottles of Monbazillac. It is eleven in the morning.

A young, handsome man is selling a little old lady with

hardly any hair a piece of sausage and a hunk of country bread. It is a courtship. He explains the unique and incomparable merits of this particular glorious sausage and this bread, all while flattering her outrageously. The transaction is consummated. They both beam with joy. They thank each other a dozen times, and he says *"Zut alors."*

It's a truism that the experience of other cultures gives you a fresh perspective on your own. No North American woman who has spent even a day or two in Europe can fail to be struck by the gender differentiation that is still allowed—celebrated, even—among the middle classes, and by the public intimacy that's taken for perfectly normal behaviour. Men are meant to be admiring and women to be admirable, and they both work hard at it.

Our own Protestant culture, like our language, has always been uninflected. The uncertain, perilous relations between the sexes have made it worse. Women have learned to dampen down any public expression of girliness so that they will be taken seriously. Men have learned to not touch, not compliment and not flirt, because it's downright dangerous. In a pluralistic culture, where seduction (like raw cheese) is considered a crime and nobody understands the rules of engagement anymore, it's best not to engage at all.

Unlike us, French women are allowed to be both stunningly sexy and serious at the same time. If you doubt it, just look at Quebec, where all the powerful women in business and politics and intellectual life are also powerfully feminine. Whenever you meet them it strikes you that they must have fabulous love lives. The powerful women of English Canada rarely inspire such speculation.

There are many other reasons to envy French women. They are born with a natural ability to accessorize. They are encouraged to be middle-aged. They can carry their little dogs with them to the very best restaurants, and they are not obliged to stoop and scoop.

Best of all, French women are not obliged to join the cult of physical exercise. In France, failing to get on the Stairmaster each morning is not a moral lapse or a character flaw, and getting sweaty is not done. French women prefer to pursue slimness by more refined means, such as the application of costly reducing lotions and little machines that electrically stimulate your thighs. Instead of spending all their free time at the gym, sweating and wrecking their knee joints, they spend all their free time at the cafés, smoking and drinking espresso. Then they go out to dinner and eat like horses. So far as I can tell, their system works as well as ours and is a lot more fun.

The ardent sensuality of everyday life in France is as much of a shock to the Canadian system as steady spring sunshine. *"Que desirez-vous aujourd'hui?"* asks the charming man who runs the tiny village *épicerie*, with its seven kinds of fragrant chèvre. In France the language of desire applies to everything, even to grocery shopping, and all transactions are a seduction. By the time we have finished discussing the cheese, he's made me feel as interesting as Jeanne Moreau.

By the third time we drop in at the village café (called *Le Temps Perdu*), the gorgeous woman in charge tells us we are *très, très charmants* and *agréables*. When we say goodbye, she embraces us warmly and kisses us three times each.

One day at the market I bought a straw hat with a big brim

and a black band. It made me feel just like Gigi. *"Ooh la la,"* murmured a handsome Frenchman as I passed.

I thought they only said that in Maurice Chevalier movies. But I was wrong.

Advice for the War on Fat: Surrender!

It's tough to be me these days. Always a pleasingly plump person, I seem to be spreading over the line to something worse. I blame my hormones, my lack of character, my ancestors. Whatever the cause, my body-mass index is approaching twenty-five.

In case you need reminding, your BMI is your weight in kilograms divided by your height in metres squared. A BMI of twenty-five means that, according to Health Canada, you are officially overweight. When you hit thirty, you are officially obese. Not just fat, but really, really fat. You don't want to go there.

Obesity is an epidemic. Nearly half of all Americans are overweight. In Canada, 32.5 per cent of us are overweight and 14.9 per cent are obese. Fat is a major health hazard, and I owe it to myself and my nation to get a grip. My doctor says so (although, to tell the truth, he's no Mr. Svelte himself). And every public health official says so.

One person who doesn't say so is Paul Campos, a law professor at the University of Colorado who made a study of the data on obesity. He's written a book about his findings, called *The Last American Diet.* "The obesity industry relies on systematic distortion and outright fabrication of evidence," he says. "It's a huge scandal as far as I'm concerned."

You can't imagine how pleased I was to talk to him.

For the record, Professor Campos has a BMI of twenty-five. That makes him a borderline fatty too, even though he runs forty miles a week and has a cardiovascular system that's in tip-top shape. "But the public health industry doesn't make these distinctions. It says that if you've got a BMI of thirty, you're obese."

Professor Campos and I are in terrific company. According to the BMI, even Brad Pitt is too fat. "Russell Crowe is very close to obese. So is George Clooney. He's got a BMI of thirty," he told me.

Not only is the BMI a scam, he argues, but so is most of the alleged obesity threat. Despite what you've been told, there is no correlation between your ordinary run-of-the-mill obesity and heart disease, cancer, hypertension and other life-threatening conditions. "Hypertension is more common among fat people than thin people," he says, "but thin people are 2.5 times more likely to suffer a fatal heart attack." Thin people are also more likely to get cancer. The only major disease with a clear link to obesity is type-2 diabetes.

A conversation with Professor Campos can perk a plump person right up. "There is literally no evidence that a woman of average height who weighs 145 pounds should lose weight for the sake of her health," he believes.

There's also no evidence that people can lose weight and keep it off. On the contrary—most people who try to lose weight end up weighing more than they did before. "The biggest myth, or lie, is that we know how to make fat people thin. We don't. But the more we prove that what we're doing doesn't work, the more the government and medical establishment tell us to try harder."

This delusion is a splendid boost for the vast and lucrative weight-loss industry, which Professor Campos calls a fifty-billion-a-year racket. I myself have contributed thousands to it. He believes our fixation with fat is a metaphor for all kinds of cultural anxieties and fears. It also allows us to express a set of prejudices that are socially acceptable. Health is just a smokescreen for demonizing fat people. Condemning them as unhealthy allows us to disguise our true opinion, which is that they are also lazy, dirty, disgusting and have no self-discipline. Like smoking, fat functions as a class marker. It's lower class.

In other words, we're a culture of fatcists.

The thought leaders of the obesity industry (who are generally white, liberal, professional-class types with BMIs under twenty-five) would be offended at this notion. But they are squarely in a long tradition of reformers who seek to improve the morals of the lower orders for their own good. They are no different from the do-gooders who tried to close down the gin mills and impose Prohibition.

This brings us to the real reason people are so desperate to lose weight. They don't really give a damn about their health, as any teenage girl who takes up smoking to stay slim will tell you. They want other people to approve of them. The need for social approval is among the strongest needs we have.

Professor Campos once did a survey asking people (mostly women) whether they'd be willing to give up five years of their lives if they could live that life at their ideal weight. Eighty-eight per cent said yes.

Actually, it sounds like an okay deal to me. It sure sounds lots more pleasant than staying on a 1,200-calorie diet for the rest of my life. By the way, my ideal weight is 112.

Chapter Thirteen

If We're So Rich,
Why Aren't We Happy?

If you ever want to know where the economy is going, just call me. I am what economists call one of your leading indicators. Just before each recession, it's my habit to take a plunge into enough debt to choke a horse. Several years ago, financial freedom could have been ours. Instead, like good modern consumers, we chose to live on the knife-edge of anxiety and desire and made the ultimate useless acquisition—a piece of country property.

Who needs fifty acres of buckthorn with a view? Nobody. But that didn't stop us. Once upon a time, I used to think how pleasant life would be after I had acquired all of its necessities. Once upon a time, I thought that when I had the house, the car, the stereo and maybe just one simple pair of Manolos, I would stop spending money and be content. And if I had any money leftover, I would give it to poor people.

That day has never come.

I've learned that Abraham Maslow got it wrong. The eminent psychologist thought that once we satisfied our basic need for food, clothing and shelter, we would seek a higher happiness through art, human fellowship and the life of the mind. Spiritual transcendence would be the ultimate payoff of prosperity. But it hasn't worked out that way. Instead, everyone would rather go shopping.

When my husband was a newborn (not so long ago), his parents took him home to their tiny one-room flat and put him in a dresser drawer to sleep. They had no car and no TV and no vacations in Florida, never mind a foreign nanny or a padded stroller or funny little outfits from Baby Gap. But they didn't mind. Neither did anyone else. They never even knew they were poor. Today, their neighbours would accuse them of child neglect.

Our unending lust for stuff is also known as the "upscaling of lifestyle norms." It means that your desires increase in lockstep with the earnings curve. Upscaling is why you need a digital camera and a high-speed Internet line, granite countertops, an SUV with leather seats, cellphones for the kids and lots of other essential items that hadn't been invented ten years ago. Acquiring and servicing these things is stressful. Therefore, you will also require various stress-relieving activities (winter cruise, massage therapy) as an antidote to the stressed-out, busy life you lead. If your neighbours have these things and you don't, you will feel even more stressed out.

People on the left say the consumption spiral is a vice. It shows that we are merely slaves to materialistic capitalism and the empty lifestyle promises of Coke and Nike.

People on the right say the consumption spiral is a virtue. It demonstrates the glorious triumph of the market system, which now offers consumers an infinite array of choice. The hearts of economists soar when we are confident and sink when we are not. So long as we keep consuming, there will be no crash, and Nortel will recover, and the factories will stay open, and we'll keep our jobs. According to them, consumption is not just a personal pleasure, but a national, even global, necessity.

But what about the people in the middle, the ones with the maxed-out credit cards? Does all this stuff really make us happier?

I'm sorry to say the answer is no. The happiness experts (yes, such people exist) claim that probably you're no happier than your grandparents were. Just the opposite. The post-war prosperity boom has delivered an epidemic of depression in all the Western nations. Are you blue? You've got lots of company. Canadians go to the doctor for depression more than for any other ailment except high blood pressure. The pharmaceutical industry is making billions inventing new psychotropic drugs to cheer us up. Sometimes shopping cheers us up too, but not for long.

There's another explanation for why we keep consuming. It's hard-wired into us. We have evolved as highly hierarchical, status-seeking animals. Consumption and display are the surest sign of status and class, and social status is essential to our sense of self. The more we have, the more we have to get to keep up with everybody else. Like low-status monkeys, low-status humans suffer terribly.

Our house in the country needs a kitchen sink. And the sink it needs is an authentic old-time country sink that costs $645. It comes with authentic reproduction country taps for just a few hundred more. It is a fine sink. Only weeks ago, I had no idea that such a sink existed, and now I have to have one.

Is this desire a virtue, or a vice? Is my sink an empty way to assuage the anomie of modern life? Is it a confirmation of my taste and style, or just a signal of my social standing, like the rump display of the mandrills and baboons? I have no idea.

Will it make me happy? Of course it will. Until I see a better one.

Helpless in Paradise: The Dumbing Down of the Middle Class

Did you do your tax return yourself this year? I thought not. Me neither. I used to, as a point of pride. But it's too complicated and takes too much time. So I gave it up, and now I contract it out.

Along with everything else.

Like all our demographic cohort, my husband and I could not function without the experts, the specialists, the freelance servants. We are the deskilled middle class, surrounded by stuff we can't fix and a physical world we can no longer master.

My spouse and I have ants and peeling paint, a mysterious bathroom leak and a car that doesn't work. We have stereo speakers we can't hook up right, and they make an awful buzz. The cat broke the fax machine. If we ever get time, we will have them all fixed by other people. Meantime, we have contracted out our home security to the professionals, which means that our alarm system goes off spontaneously in the middle of the night and blasts us from our beds.

We are terrorized by our own house.

One day our basement turned into a cesspool. Tree roots had forced their way into our old clay sewer pipes and plugged them up. Soon they would climb the pipes, shoot out the bathroom drains and attack us in our beds.

Sewers are a man's world, and my husband is a man, so he knew exactly what to do. He called a plumber and begged for mercy. The plumber sent over three strong fellows with sledgehammers and plastic pipe. They charged us only $4,785.36 for nine hours of work.

In the country, it's worse. There, the farmers and their sons make more money helping desperate weekenders than they do growing hay and corn. We found a stout young man to chop down all our buckthorn. (We know that chainsaws kill, especially people like us.) We're super-nice to him because he can pick and choose. It's a seller's market. Millionaires from Bay Street grovel at his feet. Sometimes I wonder who will rescue us when all the farmers sell out to city folks and move to Florida.

We're held hostage by our helpers. As our plumber knows.

My friends and I make our living by manipulating symbols. What we can't manipulate are tools. All the practical skills our ancestors mastered have atrophied away, like tails.

We no longer cook or clean (except symbolically). We toil

not, neither do we spin. We've contracted all that out to those more capable.

My grandmother and grandfather would have held us in contempt. Grandma (who also had a job, as a head nurse) whipped up dresses and pies from scratch. She grew fruit and vegetables in their small backyard and canned them. She waxed and polished and swept, ironed, darned and starched. Grandpa built and fixed things all by himself. He could hang a door or tar a roof or split a cord of wood in no time.

Compared with them, we're helpless as newborns.

Since their day, entire skill sets have vanished from middle-class life. Grandma tried to teach me how to sew once, but it was hopeless. Now, sewing is dead, along with Singer. For more of us than are willing to confess, serious cooking has declined into a party trick. We buy deluxe kitchens with double stoves and Sub-Zero refrigerators and granite countertops to maintain the illusion of competence.

"Well, so what?" my friend Doug said at lunch. (As usual, we paid some strangers to cook and serve it to us.) "Why should I rake my own leaves? My time is worth more than what I can pay someone else to do it."

The trouble is, contracting out has reached ridiculous extremes. There's always someone you can pay to do the chores that are too tedious or to supply the expertise you fear you lack. There are people who will clean the dog turds out of your backyard, and others who will hang your pictures more aesthetically. There are wedding planners and garden planners, duct vacuumers and grief counsellors, in case you need guidance in mourning appropriately.

In a world where everything's become professional, no one

dares to be an amateur. Why cook when gourmet take-out stores do it so much better? Why make music with your friends when they can download Mozart, brilliantly performed, any time they want? Why sing or act? Why make furniture when it's so much nicer and cheaper at Ikea? Why paint your kitchen when there are painters, or even pick the colour by yourself when there are experts with far, far better taste than you have?

We've even contracted out parenting and friendship. A huge service industry of child-care professionals is on hand to supply your kids with proper stimulation, keep them entertained at birthday parties, give them lessons of all kinds, even teach them character development.

If you fail to subcontract these experts, your neighbours and your kids will surely disapprove.

As for friends, who's got the time? We're all far too busy turning symbols into money so that we can pay all the specialists who feed us and clean us and help our kids live up to their potential and keep us from drowning in our own basement sludge. Are you feeling overwhelmed and helpless? Do you need a shoulder to cry on? Get a therapist.

Googly-Eyed over Google

One task I tried but utterly failed to delegate away was buying my own computer. This process is guaranteed to make even the most empowered consumer feel like a complete moron. For starters, computer pricing makes car pricing look ridiculously transparent. By the time you add the electronic equivalent of wheels and brakes to the basic package, you realize the prices listed in the ads are a work of creative fiction.

By throwing a dart at the ads in the newspaper, I decided to go with a major brand that shall remain nameless on account of how they help pay my salary, for which I am extremely grateful.

But then I had to choose the features. Suddenly, I had to develop preferences for all sorts of obscure things I knew nothing and cared less about. How much memory did I want? What kind of video card? Network adapter? Wireless card? Productivity software? Security system? Did I want a 24x CD-RW/DVD combo drive, or some other kind? All these things, whatever they are, came in different special deals and bundles that were impossible to figure out. I consulted far and wide and finally made my choices, based partly on what the last person I talked to thought and partly on flipping a coin, only to discover that by the time I got around to ordering the thing, those special deals and bundles had all changed.

Feeling extremely sullen, I called up the company and reached a friendly sales associate named Olivier. He talked me down off the ledge, threw in free shipping and persuaded me to buy an extra doodad called a FlashKey. He assured me I couldn't live without it.

My shiny new computer works fine. It has 58,000 features I don't need and will never even know about, and I have a nagging feeling that I've been taken advantage of somehow. But one thing has made every moment of this tedious process worthwhile. And that thing is Google.

Google has become so essential to my life that I can't

remember what I did before it existed. It can make me an instant expert on practically anything. With it, I have rented an apartment in Rome and discovered why I can't grow blue hydrangeas in our garden (not enough acid), found out where to get a Burmese cat and surveyed the recent oeuvre of rap star 50 Cent. I sneakily Googled the name of an old boyfriend to find out what he's been up to. I've checked out Janet Jackson's boob. I also found a great quote from Winston Churchill on Iraq. He called it an "ungrateful volcano," which strikes me as something I can use.

Google is like a giant communal brain, very smart and more vast than you can possibly imagine. I have no idea how it works. To me, it seems like magic.

This glorious promiscuity of information strikes some people as a bad thing. There's a lot of junk on the Internet, they ominously warn, and ordinary people can't possibly sort it out. This is elitist baloney. The genius of Google is that it makes knowledge available and easy to get for anyone who has a modem. It means we don't need gatekeepers anymore. It democratizes information and allows us to decide for ourselves.

Larry Page and Sergey Brin, the two guys who started Google, are horrified by the corporate culture of companies like Nortel. They loathe the whole idea of celebrity CEOs, like the ones who ran Nortel into the ground. Their corporate motto is "Don't Be Evil." They figure that if Nortel's motto were "Don't Be Evil," maybe it wouldn't have cut 60,000 jobs, misled investors and demolished $10 billion in shareholder value in a single day. "I guess it sounds very childish," says Mr. Brin, who wears T-shirts to work and is barely thirty, "but it's a good principle to have."

The story of the successful high-tech start-up is now one of the great American foundation myths, like the story of the baby born in a log cabin who grew up to be president. And the Google story is a classic of the genre. Two brainy computer nerds, aged twenty-two and twenty-three, meet at Stanford in 1995. Three years later they write a paper called "The Anatomy of a Large-Scale Hypertextual Search Engine." In it, they use complex math to explain how it will work. They drop out of grad school to start a company. One day at lunch they explain their concept to a would-be backer, who tells them he can't stay to hear them out but writes them a cheque for $100,000. The name of the company is actually supposed to be Googol, which means a very large number (one followed by one hundred zeros). A googol is more than the number of particles in the universe.

"You idiots!" yelled Larry Page, after some employees registered the company on the web as Google. "You've spelled it wrong." But they explained to him that Googol was already taken.

Today people use Google two hundred million times a day. It can link to more than four billion Web pages. It makes most of its money from those ads you see on the right side of the screen that say things like "Hydrangeas Plus" or "Vacation Rentals in Rome," and it is insanely profitable.

In keeping with the Silicon Valley foundation myth, Google's 1,900 employees (known as Googlers) work at the Googleplex. The corporate chef used to work for the Grateful Dead. The two founders, who hate giving interviews, live like grad students. For fun they go rollerblading. They each drive an eco-friendly Toyota Prius. They're socially conscious billionaires who want to use the company's brains and money to tackle the global problems of the environment, poverty and human rights. They think the Great Satan is Bill Gates. But because of their own market dominance, the next Great Satan may be them.

The Googlers have already shaken up the world as we once knew it. Because of Google, people like me now think they know as much as their doctors do. Libraries and encyclopedias are obsolete. We're watching less TV, reading less newsprint, because we're Googling. Google has played hell with family life. At least families sometimes watch TV together. But they Google all alone, indulging individual fantasy lives they never knew they had. Maybe your thing is sex with midgets, or maybe it's luxury villas for rent in Tuscany. It all adds up to a new social malady known as online addiction, characterized by the desire to spend more time Googling than being with your loved ones.

"Turn off that thing and talk to me," my husband barks every so often—that is, unless he's Googling for recipes for making mead.

At least I'm not guilty of that ultimate modern vice, self-Googling. This is when you type in your own name to see how many times Google mentions you. I hardly ever do this, because self-Googling is egotistical and vain. On the other hand, being Googled by other people is very nice. So Google me. Please. I'll never be as Googled as Pamela Anderson, but I can dream.

Upscale, Downscale Retail

My husband doesn't know it, but he's getting a DVD player for his birthday. The reason is that our VCR is already obsolete. The little video store we go to in the country only rents movies in DVD now. "Everybody around here has a DVD player," the owner scoffed.

I thought DVD players still cost a couple hundred dollars. But then I went to Wal-Mart and got one for $69.99. You can get them even cheaper. The day after Thanksgiving, one Wal-Mart store in the United States offered them for $28.97. When they opened the doors, a mob of shoppers trampled the first woman in line and knocked her unconscious.

Wal-Mart is where the masses shop, and when I went the other night, the store was teeming with them. They were loading up on cut-rate Frosted Flakes, Hokey Pokey Elmos and cheap electronic goods for Christmas. You could pick up a nice TV for $149. The poor are always with us, but now the poor can afford DVD players.

Lots of social critics hate Wal-Mart. According to them, it exploits its sales associates (formerly known as clerks) and pays them peanuts. It is staunchly anti-union. It's been blamed for the ruination of small-town main streets and of the moms and pops who used to work there. It has also driven manufacturing to low-wage countries. The DVD player I bought was made in China, where some Wal-Mart suppliers employ hordes of peasants who work in vast sweatshops and earn a hundred dollars a month. "Is Wal-Mart good for America?" *The New York Times* asks every so often. *The New York Times* thinks not.

The kind of people who write editorials for *The New York Times* wouldn't be caught dead at Wal-Mart. For one thing, they'd have to drive all the way to the suburbs. Also, although they'd never admit it, it's a class thing. They think Wal-Mart is tacky. They'd rather shop at Pottery Barn or Restoration Hardware, where you may not get the lowest price, but you can get stuff that will make you feel as if you live in a Ralph Lauren ad or the south of France.

I confess I like to shop at these stores, too. They stock all the newest bourgeois necessities. If your house doesn't happen to come with antiqued wrought-iron finials or crown mouldings, they'll sell you some. You go there because you want your house to reek of unpretentious good taste and refinement and you don't have the least idea how to make it do that. Fortunately, they do.

Wal-Mart succeeds brilliantly because it drives down costs and guarantees the best price. The stores catering to the modern bourgeoisie succeed because they drive up standards and guarantee the best taste. They are geniuses at selling you things you never saw before but now must have, such as floor-to-ceiling Thai silk curtains in a colour called sangria.

For all I know, those curtains are made in China, too, but sweatshop labour is not the image conjured up by the sumptuous Restoration Hardware catalogue. Instead, it evokes ancient camel caravans swaying through the desert. "Though the Silk Road began in China, Thailand is its most celebrated stop," says the blurb. "There, silk-weavers favour colours nuanced and shimmering . . ."

Who could resist? Not me. By the time I recovered from my swoon, I'd bought the curtains plus a curtain rod with wrought-iron finials and an optional set of antiqued bronze curtain rings. The curtain rings cost more than the DVD player, but so what? My husband never has to know.

The social critics at *The New York Times* blame Wal-Mart for killing off old-fashioned retailing. They should blame stores like Restoration Hardware, too. One competes on taste and the other competes on price, and stores that offer neither are doomed. Say goodbye to department stores, which offer the worst of both worlds. They're the dinosaurs of shopping, and are being driven to extinction by retail climate change.

I'm sad to say that certain fashionable friends of mine wouldn't be caught dead in a Wal-Mart store. Too bad. They should go and take a look at the single most important economic player of our time. With $244 billion (U.S.) in sales, Wal-Mart sells more of almost everything than almost everybody. Its annual revenues far surpass the entire gross domestic product of Quebec. Its DVD sales alone make it Hollywood's most important revenue generator. It is America's biggest seller of groceries, toys, guns, diamonds, CDs, apparel, dog food, sporting goods and toothpaste. It is the largest retailer in Canada and the biggest private employer in Mexico. It is a major factor in driving down the inflation rate. It has more people in uniform than the U.S. army, is growing at 15 per cent a year and is opening a store a day. If there isn't one near you, there will be soon.

And if you want to economize, it sells curtain-rod rings for $3.99.

The Horror! The Horror! (a.k.a. Christmas)

Every December I have the Christmas dream. If you're a woman, you've probably had it, too. In it, you suddenly realize that it is five-thirty on Christmas Eve, and you haven't bought a single present yet. You race toward the shops in the dark, but your boots are weighed down in the slush. Where are those stores, anyway? The streets are a maze. At last you find them, but it's too late. The glass doors swing shut in your face. You're doomed.

The Christmas dream is a variation of the final exam dream, in which you discover that you never took the course. But for me, the anxiety of Christmas is even worse. It starts the moment those irritating neighbours string their lights up in November and builds into a nerve-racking crescendo of avoidance, resentment, guilt and inadequacy. December twenty-fifth will soon be hurtling toward me like a rocket, and I haven't even baked a cookie yet.

Nor have I composed a witty Christmas e-mail letter, bought the raffia to tie around the environmentally friendly brown wrapping paper, mailed the charming handmade wooden toys to my niece and nephews, made my secret homemade chutney for the hostess gifts, invited our thirty-five best friends to a cozy open house, volunteered to serve dinner at the Sally Ann or started watering the paperwhites. I even had a plan to decorate the house with boughs and swags cunningly constructed (by me) from natural materials gathered (by me) from the beautiful Ontario countryside. If only I'd learned how.

Lots of women find time to do these things. Women who are a lot busier than me. I know women who stay up till three a.m.

making Christmas cookies for the people at the office. I long to be as thoughtful and virtuous and diligent and nurturing as they are. I think I hate them.

Instead of getting on with things, I found myself recently in a store that sells the kind of clothing you sometimes see worn in ads by models pretending to be upper-crust WASPs frolicking après-ski at Aspen. There, I went into some kind of trance, and now I own a pink woollen sweater with reindeer prancing across the chest.

"What's with those sweaters?" asked my friend Barbara, who is Jewish. She claims that all her Christian friends have one. They are only worn at Christmas and are remarkably unbecoming.

I explained to her that the sweater represents a sort of magical thinking.

If I own the sweater, then I might become a better and more competent person—the kind of person who likes to make gingerbread houses and organize jolly carolling parties, instead of the kind of person who approaches Christmas with scarcely veiled hostility and a sincere desire that, like a root canal, it will be over quickly.

A shrink would say that people who dislike Christmas have unresolved feelings about intimacy and family. If that were true, then everybody would dislike Christmas.

It's not my family that's my problem. Nor is it our society's relentless focus on empty materialism that tries to substitute money for true meaning, etc., etc. Materialism, I think, has been highly underrated as a source of satisfaction.

No, the problem with Christmas is the relentless competition for good taste, genuineness and authenticity.

The more commercialized Christmas gets, the more value sophisticated modern people place on authenticity. The more time we spend in shopping malls, the more we're supposed to deck the halls with wreaths we made ourselves from pine cones and rosehips. This explains the rise (though not the fall) of Martha Stewart. She packaged the idea of the handmade, the individual and the unique, and sold it back to us. She commercialized authenticity.

Every year, the stakes are ratcheted up a notch or two. Your status and your self-regard depend not on how much money you spend, but on how much time you invest in creating a beautiful environment. This pernicious trend is reinforced by all the women's magazines, which are chock full of clever articles showing you how to do it all yourself. To make is better than to buy, and if you buy, it's best to buy it from the maker. A butterball from the supermarket won't do. What you need to hold your head up is a fresh free-range organic capon for your Christmas dinner, preferably purchased from the person who raised it. It's six times more expensive, but that's not the point. It's authentic.

But the worst burden of Christmas is that men don't share it.

"What's wrong with a butterball?" asked my husband, who has never had the Christmas dream. His need to demonstrate the manly arts stops at chopping wood, and he has no compulsion to make or buy the perfect gift. His idea of shopping is getting sixteen gift certificates at HMV.

"Why are you so anxious?" he asks me each holiday season. "You can always get ready on December twenty-fourth."

I think I'm going to have to kill him.

Epilogue

What defines a Canadian best? It must be the lurking fear that somewhere, somehow, you might have offended someone.

We are the world's nice guys. We're likeable, well-intentioned folks, and we like to think we can get along with everyone. Other people seem to like us too—when they think of us at all. After all, what's not to like? We're the world's most successful nation, free of ethnic strife and civil war, prosperous, democratic, peaceful and diverse. Our domestic politics are noisy and complicated but inconsequential. We are multicultural, multilingual and multilateral, and we don't have any weapons.

If there's a war of civilizations on somewhere, the news hasn't really reached our shores. We think everyone could get along if they just tried, like we do. In our view, the world needs more Canada.

We think we're virtuous, but what we really are is spectacularly lucky. Our farming forebears came to Canada and discovered some of the most fertile land on earth. There were abundant markets for their wheat. The rugged individualists of Alberta hit an ocean of black gold and still act as if they created it all by themselves. Our trees and soil and minerals—and fish, once upon a time—made us rich. Yet by various accidents of history, our neighbours to the south never bothered to annex us. They went and invaded the Philippines instead.

And so we invented our foundation myths. We are peaceful—not because we're better, but because nobody ever seriously bothered to attack us. We are bicultural—because it was too much trouble to split up. The French and English, forever on the verge of an acrimonious divorce, have figured out that they're better off to share the house, and have settled into a marriage of convenience. Even though the middle classes of English-speaking Canada like to send their kids to French immersion, the truth is that our two founding cultures aren't all that interested in one another.

Our nation is far more urbanized than the United States, yet we identify ourselves with the north woods, the mountains and the wild unspoiled places we hardly ever see. We honour our war veterans and celebrate our soldiers—so long as they're just peacekeepers and they don't actually have to shoot someone.

But the greatest thing about Canada is no illusion. And that is the life it offers newcomers. It's no surprise that the most patriotic Canadians of all are immigrants. They know that those who belong to this tiny sliver of the world's peoples have won the lottery.

Like millions of immigrants who came before me, I have flourished in the soil of my adoptive land. Year by year, accident turned into intent, and now I can't imagine living anywhere else. My roots are deep now, as is my gratitude.